# PILGRIMAGE IN
# ISLAM

ISLAM IN PRACTICE

A COMPREHENSIVE GUIDE TO THE HAJJ

# PILGRIMAGE IN
# ISLAM

Hüseyin Yağmur

TUGHRA
BOOKS

New Jersey

Published by Tughra Books
335 Clifton Avenue, Clifton
New Jersey 07011, USA
www.tughrabooks.com

Library of Congress Cataloging-in-Publication Data available

ISBN: 978-1-59784-122-1

# Table of Contents

Introduction.................................................................... xi

## CHAPTER 1
## WHAT IS THE HAJJ?

What Is the Meaning and Importance of Pilgrimage in Islam? .......... 1

What Is the Evidence for the Hajj Duty
in the Qur'an and the Sunnah?..................................................2

What Is the History of Pilgrimage in Ancient Civilizations?.............4

How Was the Pilgrimage Practiced Among the Pre-Islamic Arabs?...... 12

How Was the Hajj Restored to Its Original purity?...................... 14

Why Do Believers Go on the Hajj?....................................... 17

The Wisdom of the Hajj .................................................. 21

   1- The Hajj Is an Intensive and Comprehensive Prayer .......... 23

   2- The Hajj Addresses Heart Rather Than Logic........................ 25

   3- The Hajj Is a Scene Admired by Angels................................ 34

   4- Establishing a Connection with Prophet Abraham ............... 38

   5- The Hajj Incites True Brother-Sisterhood ........................... 40

   6- Time Completely Transforms into Worship
      during the Hajj ........................................................42

   7- Places from Where the Mysteries of the Divine
      Spirit Burst Forth ........................................................43

   8- The Hajj Brings the Islamic Community Together.................46

   9- A Universally Institutionalized Assembly ............................ 52

   10-The Hajj Is Not to Stay in, But to Return Home
      with Spiritual Repletion .................................................53

## CHAPTER 2
## THE VIRTUES OF THE HAJJ

Merits of the Hajj ............................................................. 57

Complete the Hajj and Umra for the Sake of Allah ........................ 57

Virtues of the Hajj as Explained in the Traditions ....................... 59

Like a New Born Baby ........................................................ 61

Resembling the Saints During the Hajj ..................................... 62

The Hajj: A Heavenly Voyage on Earth ..................................... 66

The Sanctity of Mecca ....................................................... 68

Mecca, the Unique *Mihrab* (Direction of Prayer) of Humanity ....... 70

Some Places to Visit in Mecca .............................................. 73

The Ka'ba: Where the Hearts of Believers Beat Together ................ 75

The Ka'ba... A Luminous Column ........................................... 78

A Beaming Staircase That Elevates Us to Other Worlds:
The Journey Towards The Ka'ba... ......................................... 81

The Ka'ba: The Radiant Connection Between
the Earth and the Heavens ................................................. 85

The Place From Whence Divine Revelation Poured Down ............ 86

The Circumambulation of the Ka'ba Is Like Prayer ..................... 87

The *Sa'y* (Striding) Between the Hills of Safa and Marwa ............. 88

Supplications While Striding Between Safa and Marwa ................ 89

Incessant Effort to Find What One Is Looking For ...................... 91

Mecca Revived and Re-Inhabited .......................................... 93

Hagar Runs Frantically Between the Hills of Safa and Marwa ........ 95

The Water of Zamzam to Drink With Great Enjoyment ............... 100

Drinking the Zamzam Water for Whatever One Intends ............... 101

A Night in Mina on the Eve of the Day of Arafat ....................... 103

Mina Waits for Its Guests .................................................. 103

The Hajj Is Arafat ........................................................... 104

Arafat: A Glorious Day Spent Amidst the Angels ...................... 106

# Table of Contents

Arafat Is the Place of Imploring ........................................ 110

Moving to Muzdalifa En Masse from Arafat ..................... 112

The Standing in Muzdalifa .............................................. 112

"What Has Made You Smile, O Allah's Messenger?" .......... 113

Muzdalifa: The Blessed Place Where Salvation Is Granted ............ 115

Rejoining Mina After Arafat ............................................ 118

Mina: The Place Where Subtlety in Obedience
to the Divine Order Is Felt ............................................ 119

Remember Allah in Those Numbered Days! ...................... 120

The Place Where the Qur'anic Chapter of al-Baqarah
Was Revealed ............................................................... 123

## CHAPTER 3
## THE MAJOR AND MINOR PILGRIMAGES
## OF THE MESSENGER

The Hajj and Umra of Our Beloved Messenger ................. 125

The Messenger's Entry to Mecca and the Ka'ba ................ 132

The Messenger's Circumambulation of the Ka'ba ............. 133

The Polytheists' Intention of Tantalizing Muslims ............ 134

These People Are Like Gazelles ....................................... 135

Striding Between Safa and Marwa .................................... 137

Proceeding First to Mina Then to Arafat ......................... 137

The Standing at Arafat ................................................... 138

Leaving Arafat ............................................................... 139

Talbiya Recited on Arafat and Muzdalifa ......................... 141

"Could You Pick Up Stones for Me?" .............................. 142

The Prophet Came Back to Mina ..................................... 143

"Perhaps I Will Not Be Able to Perform the Hajj Again With You" ...143

The Prophet Offered the Sacrifice ................................... 144

The Prophet Butchered His Animal Himself ..................... 145

The Prophet Dispatched Sixty-Three Camels from Medina ......... 146

The Prophet Did the Tawaf of Visiting at Night ............................ 147

And the Farewell Tawaf ................................................. 148

## CHAPTER 4
## HOW TO PRACTICE THE HAJJ AND UMRA

Major Pilgrimage.................................................................. 149

  A. What Are the Conditions of the Hajj? ................................150

    What Conditions Are Required of a Person

    for the Hajj Duty? ................................................150

    What Are the Conditions for Performing the Hajj?.............. 151

    What Are the Conditions in Order for the Hajj to Be Valid?153

    What Does *Ihram* Mean?......................................154

    What Are the Essentials of *Ihram*?..........................154

    Specified Time ........................................................165

    Specified Places........................................................ 166

  B. What Are the Essentials of the Hajj?................................ 166

    Standing at Arafat ................................................ 167

    The "Tawaf of Visiting" ............................................171

  C. What Are the Necessities of the Hajj? ................................ 179

    Striding Between Safa and Marwa ..............................180

    The Standing at Muzdalifa ......................................185

    The Stoning of Satan (*Ram al-Jimar*) ........................ 187

    Shaving Off or Shortening the Hair ........................ 192

    The "Farewell Tawaf" ............................................ 196

  D. What are the Sunnah Acts and Manners of the Hajj?.......... 198

    What are the Fundamental Sunnah Acts of the Hajj ?.......... 199

    What Are the Manners of the Hajj?........................ 201

  What Is the Minor Pilgrimage?....................................202

    A. Description and Importance of Umra............................202

    B. The Obligations and Necessities of Umra ...................... 203

    C. The Time of Umra................................................ 203

    D. How to Carry Out Umra........................................ 203

# Table of Contents

How Many Types of the Hajj Are There?....................................204

A. Types of the Hajj from the Aspect of
Importance (*Hukm*) .................................................204

B. Types of the Hajj in Respect to the Way
They Are Fulfilled .................................................206

How Are the Hajj and Umra Performed? .........................210

Preparation for Entering into the State of *Ihram* ...................210

The Circumambulation of the Ka'ba.................................212

The Days on Which Hajj Rites Are Performed .....................215

Female Pilgrims.................................................219

Sacrificial Animals in the Hajj and Umra............................220

What are the Violations of the Hajj and Umra? .......................225

A. The Meaning of a "Violation" (*Jinaya*)............................225

B. Penalties and the Expiation for the Violations (*Jinayat*).... 226

What do the Prevention (*Ihsar*) and the Omission
of the Performance of Hajj (*Fawat*) Mean? .........................235

Is It Possible to Perform the Hajj on Behalf of Someone Else? .. 236

## CHAPTER 5
## SOME FAQS RELATED TO THE HAJJ DUTY

Can Children Go for the Hajj?.........................................241

Is Offering a Sacrifice an Obligatory Condition
in Performing the Hajj? .................................................242

Can the Sacrificial Animals of the Hajj Be Slaughtered
in One's Homeland?.................................................243

Can Money to Be Spent on Buying a Sacrificial
Animal Be Given as Charity Instead?.................................245

## CHAPTER 6
## VISITING THE TOMB OF THE MESSENGER

Visiting the Rawda at-Tahira of Our Beloved Prophet in Medina ..... 249

The Sanctity of Medina .................................................252

The Garden.................................................................................. 252

Time Elapses As If in a Dream at the *Rawda at-Tahira*.................. 255

Places to Visit in Medina al-Munawara.................................... 257

*Jannat al-Baqi* (The Baqi Graveyard)...................................... 257

The Martyrs of Uhud.................................................................. 259

The *Masjid al-Quba*.................................................................. 259

The *Masjid al-Qiblatayn* (The Mosque with Two Qiblas)............. 261

### CHAPTER 7
### HAJJ MEMORIES

Hajj Memories............................................................................ 265

The Last Hajj of Abu Hanifa...................................................... 265

Yearning of Said Nursi for Performing the Hajj........................... 269

"If I Knew, I Would Meet You"................................................... 272

The Hajj Memories of Fethullah Gülen....................................... 274

The Final Word........................................................................... 279

Bibliography............................................................................... 287

# Introduction

The word used for the pilgrimage to Mecca, a central duty of Islam, is the "hajj," which literally means "tending towards or setting out for a place." In Islamic terminology, the hajj, one of the "five pillars" of Islam, is a duty that is incumbent on male and female adults whose health and financial means permit it. The hajj consists of elaborate rites of standing at Arafat for a specified period at a particular time of the year and paying a visit to the Baytu'llah, the House of Allah, in accordance with the prescribed rites. Performed in the immediate environs of Al-Balad Al-Haram, the Sacred City, at places like the Ka'ba, Arafat, Muzdalifa, and Mina, the pilgrimage is, in fact, a holy journey towards Allah that surpasses all places, times, things, and events.

The pilgrims who set out on this blessed journey express their complete submission to the commands of their Creator, responding to His call by proclaiming the invocatory prayer, "*Labbayk Allahumma labbayk,*" which can be translated as, "Here I am, O Allah, at Your command! Here I am at Your command!" Proceeding on their journey from *the miqat*—the stations at which the pilgrims enter the state of consecration for the hajj—to the Sacred City, and reciting at the same time this *talbiya*[1] prayer of "*Labbayk Allahumma labbayk*" in an audible voice, the pilgrims actually invoke their Lord in words and actions; what they are saying is the following: "While setting out for the hajj, my true goal to reach is You, O Allah! My actual desire is You! My true love is towards You, O Allah! I am Your servant, while You are my Lord, O Allah! I am here in Your Presence, in order to offer my humble servanthood to You, O Allah!" And when this *talbiya* is chanted with enthusiasm and sincerity by millions of tongues, the entire heaven becomes full of the utmost delight and exultation, and believers benefit greatly from the mercy and blessings of the All-Compassionate.

This central duty of Islam is only required of a Muslim once in his or her lifetime. It is the first hajj which is counted as the fulfillment of this worship, and any hajj performed over and above the obligatory hajj is voluntary. As for the greatness of the prominence of this once-in-a-lifetime worship, the Messenger of Allah, peace and blessings be upon him, said: "Those who perform the hajj for Allah's good pleasure and, in the course of it, avoid

---

[1]  Talbiya, which literally means "waiting or standing for orders," is the invocatory prayer recited as part of the rites of the hajj.

all lewdness and sin will return to their home as pure from all sins as they were on the day their mother gave birth to them."[2] The hajj is such a worship that it dissolves those setting out for the pilgrimage in its atmosphere, purifies and rectifies them, and places them in the embrace of the mercy of Allah.

As for some of the wisdom and social benefits of pilgrimage, one can note that the hajj is like a rehearsal for the gathering of the Day of Judgment; each pilgrim becomes a small unit amid the great congregation of millions of Muslims that come from the four corners of the world during the hajj season. The hajj depicts a living scene of equality and brotherhood among Muslims, bringing millions of believers of all races, tongues, countries, cultures, and traditions together without any discrimination regarding level, position, dignity, or any other designation. Wearing the simple white apparel of the hajj, all pilgrims, from all walks of life—the rich and the poor, the weak and the strong—all obey the same rules, all bear the same difficulties, all move among the same conditions, and all go through a training of physical equality and spiritual brotherhood.

On Arafat, the hajj worship makes a very wealthy person who has ample possessions open his hands side-by-side with a believer who can barely earn his living, as

---

[2]   Bukhari, *Hajj*, 4.

they each put on the same simple pilgrim garment and stand on shared ground. The circumambulations around the Ka'ba, side-by-side with hundreds of thousands of pilgrims, teach people not to feel proud of their wealth, high rank, or dignity, and allow them to become acquainted with other Muslims. The hajj worship carves deep impressions in the memories of human beings which will never be erased. Thanks to the hajj, this beautiful interaction occurs between believers who come from all over the world.

Muslims who perform the hajj sincerely acquire beautiful attributes, like patience—enduring distress and difficulties with tolerance, reconciliation, cooperation, and flexibility. The hajj takes its visitors on a voyage which is over 14 centuries old. It allows these visitors to spiritually come together with beloved Prophet Muhammad, peace and blessings be upon him, and reminds them of the great efforts and struggles exhibited in those places. And at the same time, the hajj presents a scene from the Day of Resurrection, reminding pilgrims of the reality that they are but guests on this fleeting earth.

This work on the hajj is composed of seven chapters. In the first chapter, we put forward uplifting points and wisdom about the hajj. Our aim in this chapter is to find answers to all the questions that may be in the minds of people who are going on the hajj, and to provide them with the ability to perform their hajj worship in complete peace of mind and heart. In the second chapter, we explain the virtues and blessings of the hajj. Within this framework, we also give information about the virtues and importance of places where these prayers are performed, as well as discussing the virtues of the prayers performed during the hajj. In the third chapter, relying upon traditions, we visualize the hajj and *umra* (minor pilgrimage) prayers performed by Prophet Muhammad, peace and blessings be upon him. In the fourth chapter, we establish the principles, in the form of the practical rites of the pilgrimage, which a person who goes on the hajj must obey. In the fifth chapter, frequently asked questions about the hajj worship and their answers are dealt with. In the sixth chapter, the Masjid an-Nabawi (the Mosque of the Prophet in Medina) and other places to visit are discussed, and information about the manner of visiting the Holy Rawda (grave) of the Prophet, peace and blessings upon him, is given. In the seventh and final chapter, the work is concluded by giving some unforgettable memories of the hajj under the title, "Memorable Events of the Hajj."

I would like to say, with gratitude, that I have greatly benefited when writing this work, particularly in subjects related to the uplifting attributes and wisdom of the hajj, from the sermons given by Fethullah Gülen and his illuminating articles on the hajj.

In this humble work, if I am able to contribute to some small particle of the grand and universal adoration of Islam being understood and comprehended from a deeper perspective, then this is a great favor and blessing from our Supreme Lord. I pray that everyone who goes on this journey receives a "*hajj mabrur*" (i.e., a hajj graced with Divine acceptance and pleasure), and I ask, with modesty, that they will not forget to remember us in their sincere supplications.

Hüseyin Yağmur

# Chapter 1
# What Is the Hajj?

## What Is the Meaning and Importance of Pilgrimage in Islam?

T he hajj means aiming and tending towards a certain object. However, to explain this word just with these meanings would not be correct. The hajj is a holy visit made in compliance with specific acts of worship that are performed at a specific time and place in a specific way. In this respect, the pilgrim is required to enter into the state of *ihram* at a particular time of the year, with the intention of performing the hajj while standing at Arafat and circumambulating the Ka'ba, both of which are fundamentals of the hajj. This is a spiritual state of purity during which pilgrims keep away from frivolous and indecent talk and acts, abandon sexual relations with their spouses, and purify themselves of all worldly pollution. In general, all the rites attending pilgrimage are called *manasik*, and those who perform these rites are called *hajj-is*, i.e. pilgrims.

Becoming an obligation for Muslims in the ninth year after the Messenger's emigration to Medina (632 CE), the hajj is a fundamental duty to be performed for those who can afford it physically and financially. There are express injunctions in both the Qur'an and the Sunnah in relation to this central duty of Islam, and all Muslim scholars unanimously agree that the hajj is obligatory only once during a Muslim's lifetime.

## What Is the Evidence for the Hajj Duty in the Qur'an and the Sunnah?

The hajj is enjoined in the Qur'an and is, therefore, an obligatory religious duty:

وَلِلّٰهِ عَلَى النَّاسِ حِجُّ الْبَيْتِ مَنِ اسْتَطَاعَ إِلَيْهِ سَبِيلًا
وَمَن كَفَرَ فَإِنَّ اللّٰهَ غَنِيٌّ عَنِ الْعَالَمِينَ

Pilgrimage to the House is a duty owed to Allah by all who can afford a way to it (physically and financially). And whoever refuses (the obligation of the Pilgrimage) or is ungrateful to Allah (by not fulfilling this command), Allah is absolutely independent of all creatures. (Al Imran 3:97).

The rites of this Divine command are clearly established in various verses of the Qur'an, particularly in the chapter entitled "Hajj" (Chapter 22). In relation to this once-in-a-lifetime duty, the Messenger of Allah, peace and blessings be upon him, said, "O people! Allah has ordained the hajj for you, so perform it."[1]

The hajj is one of the "five pillars" of Islam, as mentioned in another hadith: "Islam has been founded upon five pillars. These are testifying that there is no deity worthy of worship but Allah and that Muhammad is the Messenger of Allah; establishing the prayers; paying the prescribed alms; observing the fast of Ramadan; and performing the pilgrimage to the House of Allah, the Ka'ba, for those who are able."[2] The Prophet himself instructed the believers in the rituals of the hajj with his own practice and by approving the practices of his Companions.

When the Prophet conveyed that the hajj had been made obligatory upon Muslims, one of the Companions inquired: "O Messenger of Allah, is it to be performed every year?" He remained silent till the man repeated the question three times. Then he said, "Had I replied in the affirmative, it would have surely become obligatory (for you to perform it every year), and you would not have been able to do it."[3] Ibn Abbas, may Allah be pleased with him, reports the following at the end of this same hadith: "Who-

---

[1]  Muslim, Hajj, 412; Nasai, Manasik, 1.
[2]  Bukhari, Iman, 1; Muslim, Iman, 20; Tirmidhi, Iman, 3.
[3]  Muslim, Hajj, 412; Nasai, Manasik, 1.

ever performs the hajj more than once, this will be supererogatory."[4] Therefore, performing the hajj once in a lifetime is compulsory upon every individual, male or female. In relation to fulfilling this central duty, as soon as one can afford the physical and financial requirements, the Prophet said: "Employ haste to perform the duty of the hajj, for verily none of you knows when death will reach you."[5]

## What Is the History of Pilgrimage in Ancient Civilizations?

Allah the Almighty made Mecca sacred and bestowed respect and sanctity upon it the day He created the heavens and the earth. In it is the *Baytu'llah*, the House of Allah, appointed for the worship of Allah on earth. The boundaries for the *Haram*, the Sanctuary, were laid in the heavenly worlds, before Prophet Adam, peace be upon him, honored the earth with his presence. Regarding this, the angels once said to the first man, "Before you were created, we circumambulated the Ka'ba many times." And long before Prophet Abraham, peace be upon him, rebuilt the House by raising it on top of the existing foundations, as guided by Archangel Gabriel, Prophet Adam

---

4   Ahmad ibn Hanbal, Musnad II, 508; Nasai, Manasik, 1.
5   Abu Dawud, Manasik, 5; Ibn Maja, Manasik, 1.

erected the first House of Prayer on this sanctified place; this is mentioned in the third chapter of the Qur'an:

$$\text{إِنَّ أَوَّلَ بَيْتٍ وُضِعَ لِلنَّاسِ لَلَّذِي بِبَكَّةَ مُبَارَكًا وَهُدًى لِّلْعَالَمِينَ}$$

Behold, the first House (of Prayer) established for humankind is the one at Bakka, a blessed place and a (center of) guidance for all peoples. (Al Imran 3:96).

It is notable that the word used in this verse for this sacred city is Bakka, one of the five names utilized for Mecca in the Qur'an.

Pilgrimage is not a strange thing for the People of the Book. In fact, it still exists in the Bible. The very answer of Prophet Jacob to the Pharaoh in the Old Testament alludes to the pilgrimage as a well-known annual event: "Pharaoh asked him, 'How old are you?' And Jacob said to Pharaoh, 'The years of my pilgrimage are a hundred and thirty. My years have been few and difficult, and they do not equal the years of the pilgrimage of my fathers'" (Genesis 47:8–9).

The Semitic languages of Hebrew and Arabic share many words in common. The Hebrew word *hag* is the same as the Arabic word *hajj*. In modern Hebrew, *hag* is used to mean "festival." The Old Testament states, "Three times thou shalt keep a *hag* unto Me in the year" (Exodus 23:14). These *haggim* (festivals or holy days) are the three pil-

grimage festivals in the Jewish calendar. These three pilgrimage festivals are *Pesach*, Passover; *Shavuot*, the Feast
of Weeks, also known as the Festival of the First Fruits;
and *Sukkot*, the Festival of the Tabernacles, also known
as the Festival of the Booths. After setting up their own
booth with fruit and vegetables, the Jewish believers come
together to eat during the Sukkot festival. Following this
Festival of the Booths hosting people for meals, they have
a great session of singing and dancing. However, the *hag*
was not originally days of celebration, but rather holy days.
In ancient times, the pilgrimage holy day was one of the
*haggim*, or holy days during which Jewish people used to
set out for Jerusalem to worship and offer sacrifices to
Allah in Solomon's Temple, which is accepted among Jews
today as the First Temple.

The Pilgrim's Song in the Bible captivatingly paints
a marvelously striking parallel picture of Mecca and the
first House of Allah which was appointed for pilgrimage
for all humanity:

> How dear to me is your dwelling, O Lord of hosts!
> My soul has a desire and longing for the courts of
> the Lord;
> My heart and my flesh rejoice in the living God.
> The sparrow has found her a house
> And the swallow a nest where she may lay her young;
> By the side of your altars, O Lord of hosts,
> My King and my God.

# What Is the Hajj?

Happy are they who dwell in your house!
They will always be praising you.
Happy are the people whose strength is in you!
Whose hearts are set on the pilgrims' way.
Those who go through the desolate valley will find
it a place of springs,
For the early rains have covered it with pools of water.
They will climb from height to height,
And the God of gods will reveal himself in Zion.
Lord God of hosts, hear my prayer;
Hearken, O God of Jacob.
Behold our defender, O God;
And look upon the face of your Anointed.
For one day in your courts is better
Than a thousand in my own room,
And to stand at the threshold
Of the house of my God
Than to dwell in the tents of the wicked.
For the Lord God is both sun and shield;
He will give grace and glory;
No good thing will the Lord withhold
From those who walk with integrity.
O Lord of hosts,
Happy are they who put their trust in you!
(Psalms 84:1-12)

The opening lines depict for us those blessed people who have an extraordinary yearning to set out for the pilgrimage to the House of Allah. Though Allah favored some lands over others, venerating such places as Mecca,

Medina, and Jerusalem, the "House of Allah" mentioned in this Biblical psalm obviously refers to the First House in Mecca, which lies in a "desolate valley" surrounded by the rocky mountain ranges of Paran. The parallel translation in the King James Bible paints still a clearer picture by even providing the name of this "desolate valley" as "Baca," a transliteration for "Bakka" in English:

> Blessed are they that dwell in thy house:
> They will be still praising thee. Selah!
> Blessed is the man whose strength is in thee;
> In whose heart are the ways of them.
> Who passing through the valley of Baca make it a well;
> The rain also filleth the pools.
> (Psalms 84:3-5)

Accordingly, the Pilgrim's Song describes the high status of Baca and the virtues of its dwellers and visitors. And those who set out on "the pilgrim's way" (Psalms 84:4), passing through this sanctuary in the desolate valley, "will always be praising" (Psalms 84:3) the Creator and Lord of us all. This perpetual praising of the Lord of the worlds, during pilgrimage in this desolate valley, alludes to the permanence of this Divine duty of pilgrimage to Bakka. In fact, one of the rites of pilgrimage to be performed is clearly depicted in the psalm as, "climbing from heights to heights" (Psalms 84:6). This could well refer to sa'y, the striding back and forth seven times between the hills of Safa and Marwa in Mecca. The pilgrims, who climb from Safa to Marwa, stand at each hill and recite each time, إِنَّ الصَّفَا وَالْمَرْوَةَ مِن شَعَائِرِ اللهِ *"Safa and Marwa are among the signs of Allah..."* (al-Baqarah 2:158). Certain signs, *shi'ar*, such as the houses of prayer, congregational prayers at such facilities, and the hajj with its rites, are all public symbols that identify Islam. It is the First House of Allah, first and foremost, and the *Haram*, or sacred environs of Mecca, where the signs and manifestations of Allah the Almighty are revealed during the hajj season.

The origin of this rite of *sa'y* goes back to the events in the life of the family of Prophet Abraham who, upon a Divine command, took his wife, Hagar, and infant son, Ishmael, into what the Qur'an calls the بِوَادٍ غَيْرِ ذِي زَرْعٍ عِندَ بَيْتِكَ *"uncultivable valley by Thy Sacred House,"* (Ibrahim 14:37) in Mecca, in order to settle them there. The Bible also mentions in detail that the wilderness of Paran is the area in the desert where, upon the order of God, Hagar was left by her husband, Abraham, to live with her son, Ishmael (Genesis 21:14–21).

Searching for water to quench Ishmael's thirst in this uncultivable valley, Hagar ran back and forth seven times between these two rocky hillocks. She did not simply wait for a miracle, but rather put her trust in Allah and tried to find water in the desolate desert valley, without losing hope. The water gushed forth miraculously from an unexpected place: under Ishmael's feet. That place, known as the well of Zamzam, is also spoken of the Authorized Version of the Psalms:

Who passing through the valley of Baca make it a well;
The rain also filleth the pools.
(Psalms 84:5)

Passing traders and nomads joined Hagar and Ishmael to settle in this desolate desert valley, and over time,
the small settlement grew into the city of Mecca. Since
the days of Hagar, the mother of Prophet Ishmael, the
Zamzam well has continued to flow incessantly to meet
the needs of millions of pilgrims, visitors, and residents.

As for the manifold reward and special reverence
given to this sacred place, the Biblical psalm expresses:

For one day in your courts is better
Than a thousand in my own room,
And to stand at the threshold
Of the house of my God
Than to dwell in the tents of the wicked.
(Psalms 84:9)

This prominent position and rank of the "courts" and
of "the threshold of the house of my Allah" in the Biblical verse has considerable parallels with the following
Hadith: "A prayer in the Masjid al-Haram (the Sacred
Mosque) is better than one hundred thousand prayers
(anywhere else)." Thus, prayers there are far superior in
reward to prayers made anywhere else in the world. The
hadith also indicates that the reward for every good deed
in the Masjid al-Haram, or the Sacred Mosque, is multi-

ple. In relation to the sanctity of the Ka'ba, the Qur'an states that, جَعَلَ اللهُ الْكَعْبَةَ الْبَيْتَ الْحَرَامَ قِيَامًا لِّلنَّاسِ "*Allah has made the Ka'ba, the Sacred House, an asylum of security and benefits for humankind*" (al-Maedah 5:97). The atmosphere of peace and the inviolability of this sacred place are also referred to in the Psalms:

> The sparrow has found herself a house
> And the swallow,
> A nest where she may lay her young-
> By the side of your altars,
> O Lord of hosts,
> My King and my God.
> (Psalms 84:2)

Any act of violence, like killing an animal or game, even speaking of killing a human being, or cutting any green grass or trees in the sacred precincts of Mecca, is *haram*, in conformity with the command of not violating the sanctity of this place. Thus, if someone in a state of consecration, known as *ihram*, kills an animal, then he or she should make an expiatory donation to charity. The objective of such hajj rites and restrictions is to submit to Allah's orders wholeheartedly, to create an atmosphere of peace, and to help the minds of the pilgrims become spiritually inclined.

From all these, we can deduce that the pilgrimage to the House of Allah is not unique to Muslims, but also common to all Abrahamic faiths, as the present versions of the Bible speak visibly of the pilgrimage to be observed with its rites, even though, in practice, it has been lost over time.

## How Was the Pilgrimage Practiced Among the Pre-Islamic Arabs?

The origin of the Divinely prescribed pilgrimage goes back to Prophet Abraham, who taught the sacred rites of hajj as we know them today. The Qur'an indicates the permanence of this Divine command with its current rites in Chapter 22, entitled "Hajj," where it speaks of the Prophet Abraham's calling of people to perform the hajj:

وَإِذْ بَوَّأْنَا لِإِبْرَاهِيمَ مَكَانَ الْبَيْتِ أَن لَّا تُشْرِكْ بِي شَيْئًا
وَطَهِّرْ بَيْتِيَ لِلطَّائِفِينَ وَالْقَائِمِينَ وَالرُّكَّعِ السُّجُودِ

Remember when We assigned to Abraham the site of the House (Ka'ba) as a place of worship, (directing him): "Do not associate any partners with Me in any way, and keep My House pure (from any material and spiritual filth) for those who will go round it in devotion, and those who will stand in prayer before it, and those who will bow down and prostrate themselves in worship. (Al-Hajj 22:26).

During their lifetimes, Prophets Abraham and Ishmael, peace be upon them, maintained the hajj; however, gradually, with the passage of time, the hajj rites were distorted and lost their meaning. And people abandoned the Prophet Abraham's teachings of worshipping One Allah without associating any partners with Him. As polytheism spread throughout Arabia, idols were placed in and around the Ka'ba. Its walls became covered with poems and paintings, and eventually over 360 idols came to be placed in and around the Ka'ba. Worship became devoid of the sincere remembrance of Allah and descended into the worship of many gods and goddesses. The religious rite of circumambulating the Ka'ba was reduced to a festival. The pilgrims held poetry competitions praising the bravery and magnificence of their own tribesmen, and they sang and danced naked around the Ka'ba, arguing that they should appear before Allah in the same condition that their mothers gave birth to them. In addition, they distorted the rite of sacrificing animals during the hajj. The chief of each tribe gave grand feasts, sacrificing numerous animals so that they could become famous for their generosity. With the belief that they were dedicating the flesh and blood of some sacrificial animals to Allah, they poured the blood of these animals over the walls of the Ka'ba and hung their flesh from pillars around it. For centuries, they followed these mistaken traditions of their forefathers, distorting beliefs and practices for a trifling price, such as worldly benefit, status, and renown.

# How Was the Hajj Restored to Its Original purity?

After the acts of the worship of the hajj had long been stripped of any real meaning, and all its rites had been distorted, Allah the Almighty eventually sent down another Prophet, one last time answering the supplication of Prophet Abraham, peace be upon him:

رَبَّنَا وَابْعَثْ فِيهِمْ رَسُولًا مِنْهُمْ يَتْلُو عَلَيْهِمْ آيَاتِكَ وَيُعَلِّمُهُمُ الْكِتَابَ وَالْحِكْمَةَ وَيُزَكِّيهِمْ ۚ إِنَّكَ أَنتَ الْعَزِيزُ الْحَكِيمُ

Our Lord! Raise up among them a Messenger of their own, reciting to them Your Revelations, and instructing them in the Book (that You will reveal to him) and the Wisdom, and purifying them (of false beliefs and doctrines, of sins and all kinds of uncleanness). Surely You are the All-Glorious with irresistible might, the All-Wise. (Al-Baqarah 2:129).

The *Wisdom* in this verse refers to the ways of understanding the Book and the ways of practicing or applying it in daily life. In this meaning, "the Wisdom" is almost synonymous with the Sunnah of the Messenger. Express injunctions were revealed to the Prophet to purify the hajj rites from all adulterations and alterations. As the foremost and greatest interpreter of the Book, Prophet Muhammad, peace and blessings be upon him, provided detailed explanations of the same religious decrees that Prophet Abraham and all the other Prophets, peace be upon them, came with, and smashing the idols like Prophet Abraham, he restored the Ka'ba and the hajj rites to their original purity.

The day the blessed Prophet conquered Mecca, he ordered that the Ka'ba be cleared of all paintings and idols. Among those idols were one for Abraham and another for Ishmael, each carrying divining arrows in their hands. As narrated by Ibn Abbas, may Allah be pleased with him:

> When the Messenger of Allah saw the pictures in Ka'ba he did not enter it until they had been wiped off. When he saw the idols of Abraham and Ishmael carrying arrows of divination, he said, 'May Allah punish them (i.e. the people who have made them)! By Allah, neither Abraham nor Ishmael practiced divination with arrows.

The noble Prophet put an end to all pre-Islamic misguided customs of polytheists as he said, "No polytheist is allowed to perform the hajj after the current year, nor will any naked person be allowed to circumambulate the House (the Ka'ba)." Indecency was strictly banned with the following verse:

$$
\text{قُلْ مَنْ حَرَّمَ زِينَةَ اللهِ الَّتِي أَخْرَجَ لِعِبَادِهِ وَالطَّيِّبَاتِ مِنَ}
$$

$$
\text{الرِّزْقِ ۚ قُلْ هِيَ لِلَّذِينَ آمَنُوا فِي الْحَيَاةِ الدُّنْيَا خَالِصَةً}
$$

$$
\text{۞ يَوْمَ الْقِيَامَةِ ۗ كَذَلِكَ نُفَصِّلُ الْآيَاتِ لِقَوْمٍ يَعْلَمُونَ}
$$

$$
\text{قُلْ إِنَّمَا حَرَّمَ رَبِّيَ الْفَوَاحِشَ}
$$

*"Say: 'Who is there to make unlawful the adornment (i.e. clothes) that Allah has brought forth for His servants?' ... Say: 'My Lord has made unlawful only indecent, shameful deeds...'"* (al-A'raf 7:32–33), and all evil, in words and deeds, was forbidden during the hajj:

$$ الْحَجُّ أَشْهُرٌ مَّعْلُومَاتٌ ۚ فَمَن فَرَضَ فِيهِنَّ الْحَجَّ $$
$$ فَلَا رَفَثَ وَلَا فُسُوقَ وَلَا جِدَالَ فِي الْحَجِّ $$

*"Whoever undertakes the duty of hajj in them (i.e. the well-known months), there is no sensual indulgence, nor wicked conduct, nor disputing during the hajj"* (al-Baqarah 2:197). The pilgrims submit themselves to Allah's commands full of humility in their simple white apparel of the ihram. Shedding tears and asking for Allah's forgiveness, they spend their time in worship and supplication, with neither festivals nor entertainment.

The Messenger also prohibited the slaughtering of animals for fame or worldly status. The pilgrims are ordered, instead, to offer sacrifices in the Name of Allah, and to seek His good pleasure only:

$$ وَالْبُدْنَ جَعَلْنَاهَا لَكُم مِّن شَعَائِرِ اللهِ لَكُمْ فِيهَا خَيْرٌ $$
$$ فَاذْكُرُوا اسْمَ اللهِ عَلَيْهَا صَوَافَّ $$

*"And the cattle (including especially the camels), We have appointed their sacrifice as among the public symbols and rit-*

*uals set up by Allah for you, in which there is much good for you. When they are lined up in standing position for sacrifice, pronounce Allah's Name over them"* (al-Hajj 22:36). The pre-Islamic custom of pouring the blood of sacrificial animals on the walls of the Ka'ba and hanging their flesh around it was abolished:

$$لَن يَنَالَ اللّٰهَ لُحُومُهَا وَلَا دِمَاؤُهَا وَلٰكِن يَنَالُهُ التَّقْوٰى مِنكُمْ كَذٰلِكَ سَخَّرَهَا لَكُمْ لِتُكَبِّرُوا اللّٰهَ عَلَىٰ مَا هَدَاكُمْ$$

*"(Bear in mind that) neither their flesh nor their blood reaches Allah, but only piety and consciousness of Allah reach Him from you. We have put them in your service so that you must exalt Allah because He has guided you (to correct belief and worship and obedience to Him)"* (al-Hajj 22:37). After putting an end to all misguided customs from the pre-Islamic era, all the rites of the hajj were restored to their original purity with only piety, austerity, and true worship and remembrance of Allah in mind and action.

## Why Do Believers Go on the Hajj?

We go on the hajj because our Lord, Allah, commands us to do so. We go on the hajj in order to fulfill the order of Our Lord, Who has created us in the best and perfect form and Who constantly grants us uncountable blessings and bounties—Who has created us so that we will know Him and worship Him.

When something is performed solely because Allah has commanded it to be done, then this deed becomes worship. Hence, we should perform acts of worship with great sincerity merely to attain the pleasure and consent of our Lord, Who has commanded us to perform these acts of worship. An act of worship that is performed with the consideration of the attainment of some worldly benefits is no longer worship. Utmost sincerity in worship is very prominent, and *ikhlas*, sincerity, is performing something for no ulterior motive, but solely because our Lord has commanded it to be so; we must perform this action in no other way but in the form that He has ordered. To expect some worldly benefits from worship is never right, and such expectations seriously destroy the spirit of worship and prayers. Our Lord demands that we fulfill our righteous deeds only to seek His good pleasure. Nevertheless, Allah the Almighty placed some wisdom inside these acts of worship and, hence, encourages and motivates us to perform them. There is immeasurable wisdom in the hajj. The hajj is a form of worship that is embroidered with thousands of profound facts.

The hajj is a kind of worship in that it includes thousands of intricate meanings. While we are performing the hajj, we encounter many events that we have never experienced before. Perhaps, at first glance, we cannot grasp the meaning of, or the wisdom behind, these events. We must initially express only that the worship of the hajj is an act of adoration, where the heart and spirit are more forward than the rational mind, and which allows for the heart to be unveiled and discovered. Because of this, while we are performing this worship, we must try to illuminate and enrich the beauties within our hearts. In matters that our mind cannot at first understand, we must not straightaway dive into the path of criticizing. While fulfilling the commands of Allah, the Most Merciful of the merciful, in sincere obedience, on the one hand, we must also try to understand the inner meanings of this worship on the other, and deeply enjoy the sweet moments of our hearts, feeling the utmost closeness to our Lord. While performing this worship, for instance, in places called *miqat*, the boundaries of the sacred area, we dress in the *ihram*, the pilgrimage garment that consists of two pieces of white material; while in another place, we spend the night wearing this garment without any pillows, blankets, or soft beds; yet in another place, we stone a column made up of rocks; and in another place, we circumambulate a square construction made of stones... Sometimes we comprehend the meaning and wisdom of all these things and sometimes we cannot. Sometimes we feel the Divine intuitions and secrets that emanate from a long distance and strike our inner conscience, yet at other times we cannot. Even when we feel them, we sometimes cannot realize what they actually are.

In the sacred precincts where we perform these acts of worship, we actually feel and experience the beauty of submitting ourselves to our Lord Who has commanded us to perform these acts of worship. This submission bestows such a deep tranquility and joy because one is in the presence of Allah; humankind can never achieve such a delight through any logical deductions that are the result of mere intelligence. For example, trying to find logical explanations for the *manasik*, the rites of the hajj, like standing at Arafat on the hot sands and offering supplications there, spending the night of Eid in the valley of Muzdalifa in sincere prayer and supplication, may cause us to miss out on the spiritual uplifting. On the other hand, while practicing the rites of the hajj, if we pour ourselves into the atmosphere of full submission to the commands of our Lord, then we will be able to experience the presence of Allah to our hearts' content.

In this blessed voyage, during which the heart and soul, rather than the rational mind, will be discovered and developed, an individual who falls in love with Allah, the Ultimate Truth and Ever-Constant, will throw stones at a column made of rocks and realize that they are stoning their own lower self. When throwing the stones they will think: "I have had the honor of being created as an intelligent being; I cannot understand the real wisdom behind throwing stones at a pillar. However, there is something that my mind can grasp; it is the truth that all these things are the orders of my Lord. I feel the pleasure of fulfilling the commands of my Lord deep inside, and am thrilled with the excitement of this fact. Oh my Lord, the All Powerful Lord! How beautiful it is to fulfill Your commands and how wonderful it is to know that You are pleased with these actions!.."

Here the believer will perform the circumambulations of the *Baytu'llah*, the Ka'ba, will climb up onto Arafat, will come and spend night in Muzdalifa, will stone Satan in Mina, then will sacrifice his or her animal, while also performing many other acts of worship and feeling the utmost tranquility. While practicing all these, believers will see every sacred place where prayers and acts of worship are held as a gate that Allah the Most High has opened towards His Mercy and boundless Blessings. And while they walk around these sacred valleys of mercy and say, "*Labbayk Allahumma labbayk*," they will move with overwhelming exuberance to dive into this Ocean of Mercy.

## The Wisdom of the Hajj

Since the hajj has innumerable meanings and much wisdom, to list all of them would be beyond the scope of this work. Nevertheless, we will try to focus here upon only some of the thousands of points of wisdom regarding the hajj that we can find in written sources.

The hajj and umra (the major and minor pilgrimages, respectively) cause the Ka'ba, the Holy House of Allah, to be filled with vigor and vitality which emerge from all the prayers performed in and around it. The hajj clears and purifies the soul of each human from all kinds of sins, equipping the pilgrim with genuine sincerity (*ikhlas*), opening the doors to a new life, strengthening moral and spiritual attributes, and reinforcing his or her trust in Divine Mercy and Forgiveness.

The hajj strengthens the faith (*iman*) and helps a person to renew his or her pledge to Allah. The hajj delivers repentance that is very strong and determined (*nasuh*), and which is very hard to destroy. It purifies our inner selves and sharpens our senses, granting these wings to fly.

The hajj also reminds the believer of the magnificent past of Islam. It reminds us of the self-sacrificing and brave deeds and actions of our Prophet, who illuminated the entire world with his beautiful morality and behavior, his exemplary practices, and his outstanding Companions. The hajj, on the other hand, with the many difficulties it entails, trains people to be more patient and tolerant, correcting them and raising their awareness of the necessity of obeying certain rules.

Because of the hajj, all the servants of Allah can offer deeper and more sincere thanks to their Lord. They find a better opportunity to earnestly give thanks for their blessings of wealth, health, and self-sufficiency, which have been granted by their Lord.

## 1- The Hajj Is an Intensive and Comprehensive Prayer

Said Nursi explains the wisdom behind the frequent declaration of "*Allahu Akbar, Allahu Akbar,*" or "Allah is the Greatest! Allah is the Greatest!" during the hajj as follows:

> The blessed the hajj is a worship at universal level for everyone. Just as an ordinary soldier can participate in a special occasion, like a festive or celebration day held by a king at a military headquarters, as if he were a high-ranking officer himself, and can receive compliments and favors from the king, in the same way, pilgrims, no matter how ordinary they are, turn toward their Lord as the Mighty Lord of the whole world, like saints who have left behind many ranks. Hence, they are highly honored with this comprehensive universal worship.

> The hajj is the key that opens up many degrees of the Divine universal Lordship's manifestation to the pilgrims. It reveals horizons of Divine Grandeur that they otherwise would not see. The ensuing awe and amazement, feelings of majesty in front of Divine Lordship (caused by the spheres of worship and servanthood), and levels of ever-unfolding displays to their hearts and imaginations (brought on by view-

ing the rites of hajj) can be quieted only by repeating, "Allah is the greatest! Allah is the greatest!" And by finding satisfaction for the spirit in this way, the pilgrims can only proclaim their feelings, emotions, and joy, invigorated by what they have seen, heard, and experienced at all levels, in all degrees, and at all grades of the spiritual discovery they obtained during the hajj with the words, "Allah is the greatest! Allah is the greatest!"

After the hajj, this meaning is found in various elevated and universal degrees in such prayers as the religious festival prayers, the prayers for rain, and those performed in congregation and during the eclipses of the sun and moon. The importance of Islam's public symbols and rites, including the supererogatory types of worship, originates from this fact.[6]

To elucidate these statements we can say that a *hajji*, pilgrim, who says "Allah is the greatest! Allah is the greatest!" in repetition is truly saying "Oh my Allah, You are the Greatest! You are the Greatest of all! How Sublime and Great is Your Glory! I now understand Your Greatness... Being filled with the joy and the subtle delight of knowing You and reaching a knowledge of You, I want to exclaim out loud Your Greatness. I want to shout out this fact wherever I am, in valleys, by rivers, on hills and pastures, and I want to fill the whole space of earth and

---

[6]    Said Nursi, The Words, The Light, Inc., 2005, 215-16.

the heavens with the echo of this sound. Oh my Allah! I can only calm my exuberant feelings by proclaiming Your Greatness!"

## 2- The Hajj Addresses Heart Rather Than Logic

The hajj is a form of worship in which the heart and soul lead and the mind yields to them. By submitting themselves to the heart and the soul, the mind and logic are also able to obey Divine commands. In this matter–perhaps as is the case for many other acts of worship–the heart and the soul, receptive places for inspirations that come from Allah, move ahead, and the mind follows them. Logic abandons making comments about this matter, and reason is left aside. If mind and logic find a place here for themselves, they will be occupied with their encounters with wisdom, with comprehending the necessity and prominence of prayers, and with trying to perceive thousands of forms of wisdom with just one explanation. This means that such a lofty mind attains a high rank. For this reason, before we continue with this subject, it would be better to reflect on the different situations the mind can find itself in, either embracing the revelation or falling into conflict with it.

There is wisdom in all of the deeds of Allah the Almighty. The Ka'ba is a building, and when we pray, we face the Ka'ba; it is our *qibla*, our direction or orientation. However, it is stated in the Qur'an:

وَلِلَّهِ الْمَشْرِقُ وَالْمَغْرِبُ ۚ فَأَيْنَمَا تُوَلُّوا فَثَمَّ وَجْهُ
اللَّهِ ۚ إِنَّ اللَّهَ وَاسِعٌ عَلِيمٌ

*"To Allah belongs the east and the west: Wheresoever you turn, there is the "Face" of Allah. Allah is All-Embracing (with His mercy), All-Knowing"* (al-Baqarah 2:115). Thus, our face is actually towards Allah; and by facing the Ka'ba, we turn in the direction that best pleases Allah.

Allah the Almighty has rendered some places sacred. For instance, places like the *Masjid al-Aqsa*, the "Dome of the Rock" mosque, in Jerusalem; the *Masjid al-Haram*, the "Sacred Mosque," in Mecca; and the *Masjid an-Nabawi*, the "Mosque of the Prophet," in Medina, are some of these sacred places. The rocks and earth of the *Rawda at-Tahira* (the area in the *Masjid an-Nabawi* between the pulpit and the Prophet's tomb), where the Messenger rests, as they are so close to him, are also considered to be sacred.

The True Possessor of all properties and dominion is Allah, and He can use these in any way He desires. As Allah rendered humankind superior over the animal world, He also granted our Prophet, the loftiest of all beings in both worlds, a level higher than the angels and chose him above the angels. Allah can perform whatever deed He desires. Both honoring and rewarding, and lowering and disgracing, are in the hand of Allah the Almighty. Allah, Who has power over all, honored a stone, and this Black Stone (the Hajar al-Aswad) is now considered to be sacred. What is important for us is not the actual reason and secret why Allah blessed this stone, but rather to show our dedication to, and respect towards, whatever has been blessed and rendered sacred by Him.

## Showing Respect for the Ka'ba

As well as being a *mihrab*, a center where the hearts of all believers beat together, the Ka'ba is also the first House of Allah on earth; it is highly esteemed as إِنَّ أَوَّلَ بَيْتٍ وُضِعَ لِلنَّاسِ "*the first House (of Prayer) established for humankind*" (Al Imran 3:96). Its foundations were laid in the heavens at a time when plaster, bricks, and stones were not known, and it was constructed by Adam, the pure father of all humankind. The place where the Ka'ba was to be erected was determined long before Prophet Adam, peace be upon him, honored the earth. When the angels came across Adam one day, they said: "Before you were created, we circumambulated the Ka'ba many times."

After many centuries had passed, this building and its location were no longer visible. Prophet Abraham, the father of Prophets, and his son, Ishmael, peace be upon them both, rebuilt the Ka'ba upon the place where the original Ka'ba had stood. This fact is mentioned in the Qur'an in the following verse:

$$\text{وَإِذْ يَرْفَعُ إِبْرَاهِيمُ الْقَوَاعِدَ مِنَ الْبَيْتِ وَإِسْمَاعِيلُ رَبَّنَا}$$
$$\text{تَقَبَّلْ مِنَّا ۖ إِنَّكَ أَنتَ السَّمِيعُ الْعَلِيمُ}$$

And when Abraham, and Ishmael with him, raised the foundations of the House (they were praying): "Our Lord! Accept (this service) from us: Surely You are the All-Hearing, the All-Knowing." (Al-Baqarah 2:127).

The Ka'ba is considered to be the concrete section of the "pillar of light" from the center of the earth to the Sidrat al-Muntaha (literally, the Lote-tree of the furthest limit, signifying the boundary between the realm of Divinity and the realm of creation); humans, jinns, and angels constantly circumambulate this Sacred House. The Ka'ba is such a unique building that billions of visible and invisible pure souls desire nothing more than reaching its sacred precincts; it is possible to say that its value can be measured against the entire universe. In fact, the Ka'ba is known on the earth and in the heavens by the name Baytu'llah, the House of Allah.

Our attitude towards this Baytu'llah should be nothing but respect, for it is a structure constituted of attributes which can never be completely listed. Such respect can be demonstrated with a faith that adheres to everything which our Lord has commanded of us and rejects everything that He has forbidden. If the matter were merely a show of respect for bricks and mortar—as some people have ignorantly claimed—then the Messenger of Allah would not have bothered to destroy the stone idols that had been placed in the Ka'ba.

We can see this consideration in the following Hadith narrated by Abdullah ibn Abbas, may Allah be pleased with him:

> When Allah's Messenger conquered Mecca, he did not want to go into the *Baytu'llah* as there were idols in it. He commanded that they be taken from there. They took all of them out. Statues of Abraham and Ishmael holding divining arrows in their hands were also taken out. When Allah's Messenger saw this he said: 'May Allah punish the people who made these! By Allah, neither Abraham nor Ishmael practiced divination with arrows.'[7]

The Prophet purified the Ka'ba from idols and effigies. He also fought determinedly against idolatry and eradicated all the ideas that could stem from such beliefs. In short, he informed us that idolatry would never be as strong again and would never again find support in the Arabian Peninsula. The respect shown to the *Baytu'llah* is merely because Allah desires that this construction be shown respect and that it be regarded with care. Therefore, the respect shown to this blessed building is respect to Allah.

### Showing Respect for Hajar al-Aswad (the Black Stone)

*Hajar al-Aswad*, the Black Stone, is situated in the southeast corner of the Ka'ba where the door is; the respect

---

[7]  Bukhari, Hajj, 54, Anbiya 8, Abu Dawud, Hajj, 93, 2027; Muslim, Hajj, 248,120.

shown to this stone has spiritual significance. While our Prophet circumambulated around the Ka'ba, he would stroke the *Hajar al-Aswad* when he could, and when he could not touch it, he would salute it from a distance and then wipe his blessed hands over his face. We do not know the actual reason why the Messenger gave so much value to this stone. However, we can say that this blessed stone has attained honor due to the treatment it received from our Prophet. It is as if this stone is an instrument that records the salutations and the humble servanthood which we exhibit in order to please our Lord. This is the reason why we also call this stone *Hajar al-As'ad*, which means "the Most Auspicious Stone." That is, it is the most fortunate of all stones, for it is a treasurer where promises and oaths of believers are entrusted, and it is a recorder.

There are some mysteries about this stone; it holds some subtle meanings that we do not yet understand, and which we will perhaps never fully understand. The Prophet states that this stone will testify on Judgment Day. How will this happen? Perhaps we cannot explain this fact through the science we have today, and our technology may never be advanced enough to explain this. However, there are many similar mesmerizing wonders that support this idea. For example, as the ability of speech is a miracle of human beings, who are themselves composed of non-living materials, the ability of the *Hajar al-Aswad* to testify is also miraculous. Actually, human beings are equipped with wonderful tools and organs. But we are used to them and take them for granted, so that we forget about the miracle of being human. Just as humans have memories in which a tremendous amount of knowledge and information is kept, it may also be possible that the *Hajar al-Aswad* has been created by Allah, the Creator of All Beings, with the capability of recording data. Like a discrete and incomprehensible witness, this stone is perhaps able to record the sounds and visions of those who salute it; and the data it gathers may perhaps be a testimony in the Hereafter.

When we show respect to the Ka'ba and the Black Stone, we are not contemplating them as physical entities, in fact; rather, we are taking into account what they represent. If we were showing respect to a stone, on the one hand, then would it be logical to later throw stones at a column, which is itself stone, in order to represent the stoning of Satan? At Mina we throw stones at a stone-built pillar as one of the rites of hajj, but at the Ka'ba we show respect to *Hajar al-Aswad*, another stone. From this, it can be easily understood that our servanthood is not—Allah forbid—to the Ka'ba itself or to the *Hajar al-Aswad*, but solely to Allah the Almighty.

Uma, may Allah be pleased with him, who opened new horizons for logic and rationality in respect to wisdom and the proper cause, and who was unquestionably devoted to the Prophet, once kissed the *Hajar al-Aswad* and said:

"O stone! I know that you are only a stone. You can neither harm, nor benefit anyone. If I had not seen that Allah's Messenger had kissed you, by Allah, I would not kiss you." Upon hearing these words of Umar from behind him, Ali said: "O Umar! It is not as you know; that stone has benefits as well as harms. While everybody kisses it and salutes it, they are actually entrusting it with what they did, and that stone will testify to all this in the future."[8]

The meaning of Umar's words can be stated as follows: "The stone has neither benefit, nor harm as itself, a stone. But if Allah wills, just as He creates human beings from earth, He can also make a stone talk or record events. In this way, a stone has both benefits and harm." Thus, he was focusing not on the material, but on the meaning. Both of these men, who served as Caliphs in their lifetime, show us unquestioning obedience to the commands and suggestions of Allah's Messenger, and consideration of both the rational and the spiritual.

There are many hadiths related to the virtues of both circumambulating the Ka'ba and greeting the Black Stone. Only a few of them are given below:

Abdullah ibn Umar, may Allah be pleased with him, narrates: "Allah's Messenger faced towards the *Hajar al-Aswad*, then he placed his lips on the *Hajar al-Aswad* and wept for a long time; he then left. Then he saw that Umar

---

[8] Bukhari, Hajj, 50, 57, 60; Muslim, Hajj, 248, 120.

was also crying next to the stone. Upon seeing Umar like this he said, "O Umar! Yes, this is the place to shed tears."[9]

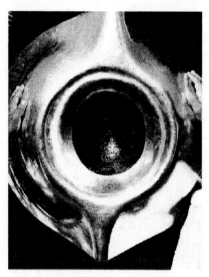

HAJAR AL-ASWAD
Allah's Messenger kissed this Black Stone
from heaven and showed it respect. How
fortunate is the one who can hold it!

Nafi, may Allah be pleased with him, narrates: "I saw Abdullah ibn Umar circumambulating the Ka'ba. He was saluting the *Hajar al-Aswad* with his hand and then he kissed his hand, (to show that he was kissing the *Hajar al-Aswad*)."[10]

---

[9]  Ibrahim Canan, Hadis Ansiklopedisi, no. 6852.
[10]  Bukhari, Hajj, 60; Muslim, Hajj, 246, no. 1268.

In a hadith narrated by Abdullah ibn Umar, may Allah be pleased with him, it is mentioned that: "Whoever goes round the House (of Allah) in a set of seven circuits and does this circumambulation in compliance with its conditions and manners, he will gain the rewards as if he has freed a slave." Another hadith is: "As a person puts one foot down and picks up the other while circumambulating the Ka'ba, for each step, Allah will clear one sin and record one reward."[11]

## 3- The Hajj Is a Scene Admired by Angels

A person who is to perform the hajj and who intends to go on the hajj must keep themselves away from *rafath* (filthy language and sexual relations), *fusuq* (wicked conduct and sinful acts), and *jidal* (quarreling and acts of violence). Behaving like this, an individual can reach a certain level in their effort to acquire angelic attributes. This matter is stated as follows in the Divine revelation:

فَمَن فَرَضَ فِيهِنَّ الْحَجَّ فَلَا رَفَثَ وَلَا فُسُوقَ وَلَا جِدَالَ فِي الْحَجِّ

"*Whoever undertakes the duty of Hajj in them (i.e. the well-known months), there is no sensual indulgence, nor wicked conduct, nor disputing during the Hajj*" (al-Baqarah 2:197).

---

[11] Tirmidhi, Hajj, III, no. 959.

The pilgrims who obey this command of Allah and perform the hajj will, for a time, become pure like angels
walking on the earth. In one respect, in this way, humankind can acquire a situation that answers the question
asked by angels during the creation of the first human,
displaying the essential character and true nature of humankind. This subject is mentioned in the Holy Qur'an as
follows:

وَإِذْ قَالَ رَبُّكَ لِلْمَلَائِكَةِ إِنِّي جَاعِلٌ فِي الْأَرْضِ خَلِيفَةً ۖ قَالُوا
أَتَجْعَلُ فِيهَا مَن يُفْسِدُ فِيهَا وَيَسْفِكُ الدِّمَاءَ وَنَحْنُ نُسَبِّحُ
بِحَمْدِكَ وَنُقَدِّسُ لَكَ ۖ قَالَ إِنِّي أَعْلَمُ مَا لَا تَعْلَمُونَ

(Remember) when your Lord said to the angels: "I
am setting on the earth a vicegerent." The angels asked:
"Will You set therein one who will cause disorder
and corruption on it and shed blood, while we glori-
fy You with praise, and declare that You alone are
All-Holy and to be worshipped as Allah and Lord?"
He said: "Surely I know what you do not know." (Al-
Baqarah 2:30)

With the statement "*Surely I know what you do not
know,*" Allah perhaps was informing the angels that they
would later witness many things that He knew and knows
but they do not, such as when human beings perform acts
of worship like the hajj. While the *hajjis* wear a simple
garment made up of two pieces of cloth, which resem-

bles the shroud worn in the grave; while they implore
with their open hands and hearts; while they sleep on
the dry earth during their stay in Muzdalifa; while they
recite "*Labbayk Allahumma Labbayk*" when walking shoul-
der-to-shoulder with other *hajjis* in the valleys of Mecca—
the angels will witness these beauties which were known
by Allah but which had been unknown by them; each
time the angels see these scenes, they proclaim: "We glo-
rify You with praise, and declare that You alone are All-
Holy and to be worshipped as Allah and Lord, O Allah!
We seek forgiveness from You for the question we asked.
You are All-Knowing and we know not!"

## We Are from the Nation of Prophet Abraham

As we are from the nation of Prophet Abraham, peace be
upon him; going on the hajj, circumambulating the Ka'ba,
and fulfilling all the rites of hajj will enable us to establish a kind of communication with Prophet Abraham. We
declare this reality at all times and in every place: "We
are the servants of Allah. We are from the community of
Prophet Muhammad, peace and blessings be upon him.
And we are from the nation of Prophet Abraham." Our
parents teach us this reality even before we start school.
During our childhood, when we were asked, "Which
nation are you from?" we answer immediately, "From the
nation of Prophet Abraham." By saying this, we state that
we are completely removed from any kind of idolatry—

that we are pure, that is, that we are *hanif*. The struggle
of Prophet Abraham, peace be upon him, against such
impurities is mentioned in Chapter Six of the Qur'an.
Trying to preach to his community, in order to show the
way to attain true belief through rational proof, Prophet
Abraham followed the same thought process as those
around him and said:

فَلَمَّا جَنَّ عَلَيْهِ اللَّيْلُ رَأَى كَوْكَبًا ۖ قَالَ هَٰذَا رَبِّي ۖ فَلَمَّا أَفَلَ قَالَ لَا

فَلَمَّا رَأَى الْقَمَرَ بَازِغًا قَالَ هَٰذَا رَبِّي ۖ فَلَمَّا أَفَلَ ۞ أُحِبُّ الْآفِلِينَ

فَلَمَّا رَأَى ۞ قَالَ لَئِن لَّمْ يَهْدِنِي رَبِّي لَأَكُونَنَّ مِنَ الْقَوْمِ الضَّالِّينَ

الشَّمْسَ بَازِغَةً قَالَ هَٰذَا رَبِّي هَٰذَا أَكْبَرُ ۖ فَلَمَّا أَفَلَتْ قَالَ يَا قَوْمِ إِنِّي

إِنِّي وَجَّهْتُ وَجْهِيَ لِلَّذِي فَطَرَ السَّمَاوَاتِ ۞ بَرِيءٌ مِّمَّا تُشْرِكُونَ

وَالْأَرْضَ حَنِيفًا ۖ وَمَا أَنَا مِنَ الْمُشْرِكِينَ

When the night spread over him, he saw a star and
he exclaimed: "This is my Lord, (is it)?" But when it
set (sank from sight), he said: "I love not the things
that set." And when (on another night), he beheld the
full moon rising in splendor, he said: "This is my Lord
(is it)?" But when it set, he said: "Unless my Lord
guided me, I would surely be among the people gone
astray." Then when he beheld the sun rising in all its
splendor, he said: "This is my Lord, (is it)? This one
is the greatest of all!" But when it set, he said: "O my
people! Surely I am free from your association of

partners with Allah and from whatever you associate with Him as partners. I have turned my face (my whole being) with pure faith and submission to the One Who has originated the heavens and the earth each with particular features, and I am not one of those associating partners with Allah." (Al-An'am 6:76–79).

When we say that we are "from the nation of Prophet Abraham," we are actually saying: "We never worship the moon, the sun, a star or any other celestial body, for all these set"—just like Prophet Abraham, who remained pure and never fell into idolatry; we announce that we are members of Prophet Abraham's nation and that we remain as pure as Prophet Abraham, peace be upon him. For we have found Al-Haqq, the Ultimate Truth, and have turned towards the One Who never sets nor can be destroyed.

## 4- Establishing a Connection with Prophet Abraham

When we perform the hajj worship we are also establishing a connection with Prophet Abraham. We render this connection in a unitary and reconciling manner as the true followers of the Qur'anic injunctions. In this verse from the Qur'anic Chapter, Al-Hujurat, Allah the Almighty says:

يَا أَيُّهَا النَّاسُ إِنَّا خَلَقْنَاكُم مِّن ذَكَرٍ وَأُنثَىٰ وَجَعَلْنَاكُمْ شُعُوبًا وَقَبَائِلَ لِتَعَارَفُوا ۚ إِنَّ أَكْرَمَكُمْ عِندَ اللهِ أَتْقَاكُمْ ۚ إِنَّ اللهَ عَلِيمٌ خَبِيرٌ

O humankind! Surely We have created you from a single (pair of) male and female, and made you into tribes and families so that you may know one another (and so build mutuality and co-operative relationships, not so that you may take pride in your differences of race or social rank, and breed enmities). Surely the noblest, most honorable of you in Allah's sight is the one best in piety, righteousness, and reverence for Allah. Surely Allah is All-Knowing, All-Aware. (Al-Hujurat 49:13).

By these words, our Lord effectively tells us this truth: "Oh, humankind! We created you from a man and a woman. Then we separated you in branches, tribes and nations and settled you in different parts of the world. By the will, the command, and the creation of Allah, the geographical conditions of the places where you have settled have caused impacts upon you and you have undergone a certain amount of differentiation. Some of you started to speak Arabic, while others learned Turkish, Hebrew, English or Russian, and yet others spoke other languages. The reason for you to be created in such a system was never to make you enemies to each other. Just as an army is separated into regiments so that its maneuver and administration can be conducted easily, you are also separated into different tribes and nations so that you will establish a brotherhood which is based upon rationality and logic and, hence, establish unity and togetherness in diversity."

## 5- The Hajj Incites True Brother-Sisterhood

The hajj is also the most fertile environment for establishing true brother-sisterhood among both individuals and nations. During the hajj, people from all walks of life—from a state president to an ordinary person, from the richest to the poorest, and from whatever geographical, social, cultural, or racial grouping they may stem—all live and move together in the same place at the same time. Groups of people who come for the hajj from different countries set up tents side-by-side and inhabit the same place for days on end. Carrying the same faith in their hearts, even though they speak different languages, they all present their prayers with the same emotions; despite their different skin colors, their different languages, their different traditions and different lifestyles, a profound unity of purpose can be clearly witnessed in this apparent diversity.

Hence, in such an environment of deep adoration, brotherhood, reconciliation and sincere intimacy, we can get a strong sense of what a universal and comprehensive faith Islam is. During the days of hajj, being completely removed from any kind of worldly worries or interests, there is nothing other than facing Allah, seeking His pleasure and consent, uniting around His Lordship and reaching the true essence of believing in One and only Allah; this can be seen in all pilgrims.

## "Labbayk Allahumma Labbayk"

For all pilgrims, there is nothing more pleasant than reciting "*Labbayk Allahumma labbayk*" during the *wuquf*, standing at Arafat. This rite of the pilgrims' stay at Arafat on the Day of Arafat is an essential element of the hajj.

While performing the hajj, groups of *hajjis* from all various countries pass by you with eagerness, excitement, enthusiasm, and profundity which you feel in their reciting of "*Labbayk Allahumma labbayk*." With all these *talbiyas* (a word signifying waiting or standing for orders), it is as if the whole world speaks in one voice, and this worship ascends to Allah: "O Our Lord, we are running towards You to listen to Your command and Your order. We submit in obedience to Your command, we declare that we are ready to become however You want us to be, and to live in the way You want us to live." In all these different voices, accents, and manners there is such a beautiful harmony that one is deeply aware of the subtlety in this declaration of the greatest truth. These sacred words are expressed repeatedly by people who, with their excitement, are like an exuberant fountain... Mountains, rocks, rivers, and hills cry as one, speaking one word:

> *Labbayk Allahumma labbayk,*
> *Labbayk la sharika laka labbayk,*
> *Inna'l-hamda wa'n-ni'mata laka wa'l-mulk,*
> *La sharika lak.*

This *talbiya*, the pilgrim's chant, which is recited or sung with a loud voice during the hajj, can be translated as follows: "Here I am, O Allah, at Your command! Here I am at Your command! You are without associate! Here I am at Your command! Yours are praise, grace and dominion! You are without associate." The meaning of this beautiful expression is very beautiful, and the inner meaning of this statement is even more subtle and elusive.

The invocatory prayer of *talbiya* chanted everywhere is the same; the affection and compassion in the eyes are the same; and the pureness of feelings in all the people is the same. Despite many diverse features, skin colors, languages and races, the spiritual opportunities of the hajj are the same for everyone. It is this beautiful expression that emanates from the mouths of believers around the Ka'ba, on Arafat, in Muzdalifa and Mina, dating all the way back to Prophet Abraham, peace be upon him, ascending to the heavens of blessings, like gentle rain falling down upon the sins of humankind, extinguishing the flames of hellfire.

## 6- Time Completely Transforms Into Worship During the Hajj

All the time, the minutes, the hours, the days and nights of those who go on the hajj are filled and enlightened by prayer. From the moment they make their intention and don their *ihram*, they are removed from all bodily desires, lusts, and appetites. Despite naturally having many desires and needs, in obeying the command of the Unique Creator, one experiences the pleasure and contentment of delaying even one's most natural needs. One puts all desires and wishes to one side, and thus tries to spend all the moments of one's life during this time for the sake of the Lord, trying to carve His name into every period, to experience the illuminated minutes of the hajj as precious seconds of time. While walking there, one feels as if one is off the ground. Sometimes, pilgrims are faced with hunger or thirst, and sometimes they are lost, losing their direction or travel companions amidst the millions of other believers. But all these worries and sorrows return the pilgrim to a different kind of pleasure—to joy and peace of mind. In all these inexpressible joyful meanings, the true meaning of the hajj is sensed in an extraordinary way.

## 7- Places from Where the Mysteries of the Divine Spirit Burst Forth

A person who has gone on the hajj also grasps another meaning: All these sacred places are the sources where Divine Revelation and inspiration pour down from the heavens, or as described by the Turkish poet, Mehmet Akif Ersoy, these are the places where "the mysteries of the Divine Spirit burst forth." These are the places from which the sad sounds of Prophet David arose and where the valleys through which Prophet Abraham, peace be upon him, passed and where the blessed footprints of Prophet Muhammad, peace and blessings be upon him, are present. Again, these holy places are where the sighs, the elegies, and the cries of the Companions of the Messenger were once heard. While going around these sacred places, there is a place that you will be shown in Badha. Just over there, they laid Bilal al-Habash down on his back and placed heavy stones on his chest, and then for days, he was dragged, tied behind camels. However, Bilal kept saying the same word: "*Ahad, Ahad!*" (One! One!) With this, he uttered aloud the uncompromising truth: "Allah is One! He is the One of Absolute Unity!"

## Every Valley Is a Reminder of an Event

There is another example of a unique valley, another notable place. It is where Yasir ibn 'Amir was martyred. Unbelievers pressed red-hot iron rods upon the chest of Yasir, the first martyr of Islam. But all the time, he incessantly expressed his inner joy and cried out, "Muhammad is the Messenger of Allah!"

After passing closer to Mecca through the valleys, each of which is a reminder of an unforgettable event, one cannot help but remember the inauspicious, terrible act of Ibn Abi Mu'ayt in which he placed camel intestines upon the blessed head of the Prophet when he was praying in front of the *Baytu'llah*. Upon entering another valley, there is a house that is now a museum. This is the house where Muhammad, the Pride of Humanity, peace and blessings be upon him, was born. The whole universe was overwhelmed by the light that emanated from this house. Shifa and Fatima were the midwives to the Prophet's mother, Amina bint Wahb. Gabriel took this house under his protective wings and the glad tidings of, "the whole universe is saved," arose from this house. This is the blessed house where Muhammad, the Praised One, peace and blessings be upon him, was born. While walking around these valleys and listening to what they say, one goes fourteen centuries back in time to witness and observe the miraculous events attending the Blessed Prophet's birth. The masses of idols have been broken, and the towers of the palace of the Persian king have fallen apart. One observes that the lake of Sawa has disappeared into the earth, that the fire of the fire-worshipper Zoroastrians, which burned continuously for a thousand years, has been extinguished. While walking around these valleys, as one witnesses the events that occurred in these places, one is filled with excitement and emotionally aroused with fervor, walking around with deep poetic feelings as if walking around paradise. In the meantime, days will elapse—but there is no realization of how many of these days have passed. Perhaps weeks will pass, but it is as if one arrived only yesterday. The hajj causes one to recall these and many other similar experiences. By setting off on a spiritual journey through the time, the traveler is shown how great the difficulties were that the believers had to overcome and how great the altruistic efforts were that they had during the early times of Islam.

## 8- The Hajj Brings the Islamic Community Together

Along with the great wisdom that is inherent in the hajj, there is also an objective of bringing the Muslim community together. This, along with many other causes, is one of the reasons why Allah the Almighty has ordered Muslims to perform the hajj. During the hajj, not only is there the joy of performing acts of worship together, there is also an opportunity for Muslim communities from all around the world to come together to discuss various matters, in diverse forums or colloquia on particular topics, bringing people representing a broad range of scholarship, perspectives, and experiences together in one place. Dark or fair, Muslims who have come from different geographical locations around the world could discuss subjects related to their nations or states and could seek solutions to global issues. For the last few centuries, however, this obligation, which should be performed along with the other rituals of the hajj, has not being carried out, and the *hajjis* are not able to benefit from such a vital and holy aspect of the hajj. Just as mosques have now lost the critical function of dialogue and leadership which they had at the time of our Prophet, so, too, the Muslim world can no longer benefit, it seems, from the hajj as a potentially very fruitful collective ground for solving the sociopolitical issues of today.

## The Severe Punishment for Deliberately not Performing the Hajj

In his book entitled, *Sunuhat*, Islamic scholar, Said Nursi, depicts some very important truths which are being experienced by the Muslims who lived in the nineteenth and the twentieth centuries:

Addendum to the Dream
The dream ended in the hajj because the negligence of both the hajj and the wisdom of the hajj incurred not troubles nor calamities, but rather wrath, deep sorrows and grief. Thus, their punishment is not the clearing of all sins, but rather an increase in sins over sins, fault after fault. It is due to the negligence of this wide-reaching and important aspect and benefit of the hajj that allows Muslims to know each other and requires the believers to establish a unity of opinion and thought, and enables their ability to engage in common efforts. This neglect has prepared the ground for the foes of Islam to exploit millions of Muslims, even turning them in ways opposed to Islam. There is India, which killed its father, thinking that he was the enemy, and which is now grieving at his head. There are the Tatars and the Caucasians who realized that they had helped to murder their poor moth-

er only after everything had been destroyed, who are now crying at her feet. There are the Arabs who accidentally killed their heroic brother and now cannot even cry due to the shock they are experiencing. There is Africa, which did not recognize its brother and killed him, and is now crying from sorrow and grief. There is the world of Islam, which without awareness and in full heedlessness, has helped to murder its own son, the standard-bearer (this honored nation that bore the standard of Islam for many centuries) and now sighs and moans out of deep pain, like a mother. Millions of Muslim believers, instead of making strenuous efforts to go on the hajj, a worship full of blessings and goodness, carry out long journeys through the world under the flag of their enemies, a situation of evil and disaster (that is, Muslims have been exploited even against Muslims on many war fronts, under the leadership and command of various nations who themselves are the foes of Islam.) Is this not an appropriate outcome to a lesson that should have been learnt?[12]

## *The Most Gratifying and Pleasurable Hajj: The Farewell Hajj*

The hajj was made obligatory in the last period of the Prophet's life, and the Pride of Humanity performed the hajj along with a great crowd. Muslims who heard that the Prophet was going on the hajj came to Mecca in groups. Everybody wanted to see the Prophet, to listen to his last

---

[12] Said Nursi, Sunuhat, Risale-i Nur Collection, II, 2002.

words, and to perform the worship of the hajj with him. The hajj performed with the Messenger of Allah was perhaps the most gratifying, the most enjoyable hajj that has ever been performed on earth. The hajj rite of standing at Arafat fell on a Friday, with Eid being on a Saturday. Our Prophet led a blissful hajj for his community and bade them farewell, saying: "O people, listen to me well, for I do not know if I will be amongst you again after this year. Therefore, listen to what I am saying very carefully and pass these words on to those who could not be present here today..." And soon after he returned to Medina, his Soul departed from this world. As a result, although this was his first hajj, it was called the Hajj al-Wada, the Farewell Hajj. During this hajj, the Prophet, the Pride of Humanity, had the Farewell Sermon and visited Muzdalifa, Mina, and Mecca, one-by-one, and said farewell to all of these places.

## The Hajj of Farewell Was a General Assembly

The hajj is a great annual meeting and assembly for not only the Islamic world, but also all Muslims from the four corners of the world. Coming from different regions in the world, Muslims go for the hajj during the hajj season and discuss the issues worldwide there. We learn again from Allah's Messenger that the hajj also has the feature of being a universal congregation of believers.

The Hajj of Farewell, the first and only the hajj performed by the Prophet (after it was enjoined in the Qur'an), was at the same time the first general meeting held with the attendance of the majority of Muslims. In this meeting, believers were once again reminded of the main principles, orders, and prohibitions of the religion. When it was noon and the sun was at its zenith, Allah's Messenger mounted his camel; he climbed to the summit of the *Jabal ar-Rahma*, the Mount of Mercy in the Valley of Arafat, and while on his camel, he spoke to his Companions for hours. Those with strong voices were repeating the sermon after the Prophet, sentence-by-sentence so that everyone could hear. Having a universal message for all times, this sermon is directed to the whole of humanity:

*"O people, just as you regard this month, this day, this city as Sacred, so, too, regard your lives and property as a sacred trust. Return the goods entrusted to you to their rightful owners. Hurt no one, so that no one may hurt you..."* The clear command of the Holy Qur'an already forbids any sins, the performance of immoral deeds or behavior that will disturb the tranquility of the society. Articulating this in simple language and giving examples with matters from the lives of the people at this gathering, the Prophet then emphasized that life and property are inviolable and sacred, 'just as this month and this city are sacred ... just as this is a place where no one can be killed or harmed, where plants cannot be cut, animals cannot be hunted or killed, and where no one can engage in warfare, except if they

are attacked... just as the rite of standing at Arafat on the Day of Arafat is sacred, etc.'

Again in his message, the Pride of Humanity said the following: "*Behold! All the practices of the days of ignorance are now under my feet. The blood feuds of the days of ignorance have been remitted. The first blood feud which I abolish is that of my cousin Ibn Rabiah ibn al-Harith, who was nursed in the tribe of Sa'ad and whom the Hudhayls killed. All dues of interest and usury that have accrued from the time of ignorance are abolished. And the first interest that I remit is that which my uncle Abbas ibn 'Abdul Muttalib was to receive. Verily it is remitted in its entirety.*"

His blessed speech continued for a long time. The sun was nearly setting. Toward the end of his sermon, the Messenger asked: "*If you were asked about me, what would you say? Have I faithfully delivered unto you the message?*" Upon this, the whole of Arafat echoed with their joyfully emotional answer that ascended to the heavens, "*We bear witness that you have conveyed the trust (of the religion) and that you have discharged the ministry of Prophethood and that you have given wise sincere counsel and looked to our welfare!*" A few seconds later, the Messenger looked towards the heavens with his enlightened and smiling face and lifted his blessed hands up, pointing his forefinger at the heavens and concluded his speech with these words: "O

*Allah! You bear witness that I have conveyed Your message to Your people. O Lord! You bear witness unto this."*[13]

## 9- A Universally Institutionalized Assembly

Our beloved Prophet institutionalized the hajj not only as a form of worship, but also as a general assembly. The hajj not only brings Muslims together, but it is also an environment where the expected behavior in relationships, negotiations, and conversations between the leader and his community is most beautifully exhibited. By negotiating some matters, by being close to his community on the top of a mountain, and by wearing the simple *ihram*, our beloved Prophet was able to teach some lessons to all Muslims about administration and governing.

Where else can one find such a beautiful scene? Where else can a person be more sincere than when he or she has been completely purified from all sins? Where else can everybody, from notables to common folk, be purged of all worldly positions and ranks, leaving behind their material endowments to stay without an apparent shelter, among strangers, wearing only the simplest attire? Where else can people be so close to each other than in Mina, where even a king waits in queue behind ordinary people while stoning the devil; or Muzdalifa, where the

---

[13] Ibrahim Canan, Hadis Ansiklopedisi, (Kutub as-Sitta), Manasik, no. 6908.

scene of the resurrection of millions of people is witnessed, or the courtyard of Mecca's Sacred Mosque, where everybody moves in close proximity and in harmony amidst a huge crowd while circumambulating the Ka'ba?...

Before the pilgrims from all around the world return with a sense of serenity for having shed their sins in the plains of Arafat, and with their hearts and minds filled with the experience of proximity to Allah, they should raise the awareness that the hajj is a grand annual assembly enabling millions of Muslims worldwide to come together each year in a spirit of universal brother-sisterhood. In this way, they will fulfill this important element of the hajj at this universal annual assembly. And in considering the future of the Islamic world, they will have a better understanding of the conditions of their brothers and sisters in Islam.

## 10- The Hajj Is not to Stay in, But to Return Home With Spiritual Repletion

The hajj is a form of worship that must be carefully performed by the Muslim community at a certain time of the year and which should never be neglected. As neglecting or not performing the hajj is a great loss to the Muslim community, so, too, does the desire to stay in these holy places, even after completing the duty of hajj, also pose a danger.

After the hajj season finishes, people of good deeds and services—despite the strong desire and longing inside them—must never contemplate staying there for a long time; these holy places are not for staying in, but for the filling of our minds and hearts with Divine inspirations and enthusiasm. In the same way that we go to the mosque five times a day, perform our daily prayers and leave; and in the same way that we attain the month of Ramadan and leave it after we have fasted for the month—so, too, we also visit these most sacred places on earth, stay there as guests for awhile and then leave. Another meaning of the hajj is that this worship is a visit. After turning towards Allah with sincere feelings and enthusiasm, and carefully performing all the rites of the hajj, we must return to our homeland and our daily lives. With the virtues and wisdom gained in these holy places, each pilgrim returns to his or her home with great warmth and with a heart that is focused on Most Compassionate Allah. They must return home so that others can also taste the beauties that they have experienced.

The owner of great sagacity, Umar, may Allah be pleased with him, from whom we learn this truth, used to hold a whip after the hajj duty had ended and would warn people, saying: "O, people of Damascus, now you must return to Damascus; O, people of Yemen, now you must depart for Yemen; O, Turkmens, why are you delaying, move towards Turkistan... and leave here!" As can be understood from the warnings of our beloved mentor, Umar, these sacred places are homes of spiritual repletion and are for the filling of our minds and hearts with Divine inspirations and enthusiasm. Those who are satiated by this great spiritual experience will set off to their destinations once they have completed their duty, carrying the light within their hearts to all corners of the world.

# Chapter 2
# The Virtues of the Hajj

## Merits of the Hajj

There are many verses of the Qur'an and hadiths of the Prophet which are related to the hajj, the sacred precincts of Mecca, and the rites of the hajj. Here, while staying within the subject of this study, we have included two verses and some hadiths, while referring those who want more detailed information to other books. We will first start with verses from the Qur'an that are related to the hajj.

## Complete the Hajj and Umra for the Sake of Allah

Concerning the hajj, the Qur'an declares:

وَأَتِمُّوا الْحَجَّ وَالْعُمْرَةَ لِلَّهِ ۚ فَإِنْ أُحْصِرْتُمْ فَمَا اسْتَيْسَرَ مِنَ الْهَدْيِ ۖ وَلَا تَحْلِقُوا رُءُوسَكُمْ حَتَّىٰ يَبْلُغَ الْهَدْيُ مَحِلَّهُ ۚ فَمَن كَانَ مِنكُم مَّرِيضًا أَوْ بِهِ مِّن رَّأْسِهِ فَفِدْيَةٌ مِّن

صِيَام أَوْ صَدَقَةٍ أَوْ نُسُكٍ ۚ فَإِذَا أَمِنتُمْ فَمَن تَمَتَّعَ بِالْعُمْرَةِ
إِلَى الْحَجِّ فَمَا اسْتَيْسَرَ مِنَ الْهَدْيِ ۚ فَمَن لَّمْ يَجِدْ فَصِيَامُ
ثَلَاثَةِ أَيَّامٍ فِي الْحَجِّ وَسَبْعَةٍ إِذَا رَجَعْتُمْ ۗ تِلْكَ عَشَرَةٌ كَامِلَةٌ
ۚ ذَٰلِكَ لِمَن لَّمْ يَكُنْ أَهْلُهُ حَاضِرِي الْمَسْجِدِ الْحَرَامِ ۚ
وَاتَّقُوا اللَّهَ وَاعْلَمُوا أَنَّ اللَّهَ شَدِيدُ الْعِقَابِ

Complete the Hajj and the umra for Allah, and if you
are impeded (after you have already put on the Pilgrimage attire), then send (to Mecca) a sacrificial offering you can afford. Do not shave your heads (to mark
the end of the state of consecration for the Pilgrimage) until the offering has reached its destination
and is sacrificed. However, if any of you is ill (so that
he is obliged to leave the state of consecration), or
has an ailment of the head (necessitating shaving), he
must make redemption by fasting, or giving alms, or
offering sacrifice. When you are secure (when the Pilgrimage is not impeded, or the impediment is removed),
then whoever takes advantage of the umra before the
Hajj, must give a sacrificial offering he can afford. For
whoever cannot afford the offering, a fast for three
days during the Hajj, and for seven days when you
return home, that is, ten days in all. This is for those
whose families do not live in the environs of the Sacred
Mosque. Act in due reverence for Allah and piety
(avoiding disobedience to Him and obeying His ordi-
nances), and know that Allah is severe in retribution.
(Al-Baqarah 2:196).

الْحَجُّ أَشْهُرٌ مَعْلُومَاتٌ ۚ فَمَن فَرَضَ فِيهِنَّ الْحَجَّ فَلَا رَفَثَ وَلَا

فُسُوقَ وَلَا جِدَالَ فِي الْحَجِّ ۗ وَمَا تَفْعَلُوا مِنْ خَيْرٍ يَعْلَمْهُ اللَّهُ ۗ

وَتَزَوَّدُوا فَإِنَّ خَيْرَ الزَّادِ التَّقْوَىٰ ۚ وَاتَّقُونِ يَا أُولِي الْأَلْبَابِ

The Hajj is in the months well-known. Whoever
undertakes that duty of Hajj in them, there is no sensual indulgence, nor wicked conduct, nor disputing
during the Hajj. Whatever good you do (all that you
are commanded and more than that, especially to
help others), Allah knows it. Take your provisions
for the Hajj (and do not be a burden upon others). In
truth, the best provision is righteousness and piety,
so be provided with righteousness and piety to guard
against My punishment, O people of discernment!
(Al-Baqarah 2:197).

## Virtues of the Hajj as Explained in the Traditions

There are many narrations about the acts of worship that
should be preformed during the hajj and the merits of
the places where the hajj is performed. Allah's Messenger said: "The reward for a hajj graced with Divine acceptance and pleasure is nothing but Paradise" and "(The performance of) umra clears the sins committed between it
and the previous umra."[14]

---

[14] Muslim, Hajj, 437; Nasai, Manasik, 3-5.

To the question "Which deed is more virtuous?" the Prophet replied, "Faith in Allah and His Messenger." When he was asked "And then which deed?" he answered, "Striving for the cause of Allah." When he was again asked, "After that which deed?" he replied, "A hajj graced with Divine acceptance and pleasure."[15]

Believers who perform the hajj have a very high value in the presence of Allah. Our Prophet explained this truth by saying, "Those who perform the hajj or umra are guests of Allah; if they present their supplications, Allah will welcome their prayers; if they seek forgiveness, He will grant them forgiveness."[16]

In another hadith, he said that, "Those who go on the hajj or umra are envoys of Allah. When they pray, Allah the Almighty immediately accepts their supplications. When they seek forgiveness and amnesty, He immediately forgives them."[17] And Allah's Messenger prayed for those who go on the hajj: "O Allah! Please forgive those who perform the hajj and those who are prayed for on the hajj."[18]

In another hadith, he gives the glad tidings, "Perform the hajj and umra in sequence. For performing these one

[15] Bukhari, Hajj, 4; Nasai, Manasik, 4.
[16] Ibn Maja, Manasik, 5.
[17] Ibrahim Canan, Hadis Ansiklopedisi, (Kutub as-Sitta), no. 6841.
[18] Tirmidhi, Hajj, 2; Nasai, Manasik, 6.

after the other eliminates poverty (due to trading) and sins, just like the bellows purifies the iron from rust."[19]

The Messenger said that one must go on the hajj as soon as it becomes obligatory upon them: "Whoever wants to perform the hajj, let him hurry. For he may fall ill, or lose his transportation, or something else may prevent him."[20]

He also gave glad tidings of the acceptance of the prayers of those who heeded the invitation of Allah and who went on the hajj: "Those who struggle on the way of Allah, and those who go for the hajj and umra are stewards of Allah. For Allah called people to fulfill these deeds and they have accepted this invitation. In response to this, they demand from Allah whatever they want, and Allah will grant them what they desire."[21]

## Like a New Born Baby

The hadiths given below indicate that a person who performs a hajj graced with Divine acceptance and pleasure will be purified from all of their sins, great or small, and that they will enter Paradise.

Whoever performs the hajj, and in the course of it keeps away from sexual intercourse and avoids bad

---

[19] Tirmidhi, Hajj, 2; Nasai, Manasik, 6.

[20] Ibrahim Canan, ibid., no. 6838.

[21] Ibrahim Canan, ibid., no. 6842.

language and wicked conduct, will be purified from all sins, becoming (as pure as) a newborn baby.[22]

Related to this subject, Qadi 'Iyad comments that, "those who follow the Sunnah of the Prophet are in agreement that the hajj can act as redemption for great sins only if the person has sincerely repented." There is no scholar who claims that a person's obligations before Allah, like the five daily prayers and offering prescribed alms, as well as their liabilities towards other individuals, like financial obligations, will be forgiven by the hajj. The rights of others upon the person who performs the hajj continue. On the Day of Judgment, Allah the Almighty gathers together all those who have rights over others and those whose rights are with others, so that people will receive their rights. However, it is also possible that the All Exalted and Eternally Compassionate Creator can please those who have rights upon us by granting them some glorious bounties on that day.[23]

## Resembling the Saints During the Hajj

Describing the hajj as the grandest form of worship, Said Nursi, in "The Rays Collection," expressed another dimension of the depth of hajj worship: "Standing before the

---

[22]   Bukhari, Muhsar, 9,10; Nasai, Hajj, 4; Ibn Maja, Manasik, 3; Darimi, Manasik, 7; Ibn Hanbal, II, 229, 410, 484, 494.

[23]   Wahba Zuhayli, Islam Fikhi Ansiklopedisi, III, 12.

universal manifestations of the Lord of All the Worlds and the Earth, and perceiving these universal manifestations in the hajj, I imagined and felt that an extensive, universal worship and servanthood must be presented in response." He thus reveals his profundity regarding practicing all acts of worship, although he never was able to go on the hajj himself due to the particular difficulties of his life:

> It was the Feast of the Sacrifice ('Eid al-Adha) when this 'station' was written:
>
> One fifth of mankind, over one billion people, declares altogether: "Allah is the Greatest! Allah is the Greatest! Allah is the Greatest!" And as if the globe broadcasts to its fellow planets in the skies the sacred words of "Allah is the Greatest!" more than four million pilgrims performing the Hajj, on 'Arafat and at the Festival, declare together: "Allah is the Greatest!" These are all a response, in the form of extensive, universal worship, to the universal manifestation of Allah's Supreme Lordship through His sublime titles of the Lord of All the Worlds and the Earth; and they are, in a way, an echo of "Allah is the Greatest!" as spoken and commanded one thousand four hundred years ago by Allah's Noble Messenger (Peace and blessings be upon him) and his Family and Companions. This I imagined, and felt, and was certain about.

Then I wondered if the sacred phrase has any connection with our matter. It suddenly occurred to me that first and foremost this phrase, as well as many others, like "There is no deity but Allah!"; "All praise be to Allah!"; and "Glory be to Allah!" Such phrases of Islam, which can be called "enduring good works," recall particular and universal points about the matter we are discussing, and infer its realization.

For example, one aspect of the meaning of, "Allah is the Greatest" is that Divine power and knowledge are greater than everything; nothing at all can exceed the bounds of Allah's knowledge, nor escape nor be saved from the disposals of His power. He is greater than the things we fear most. This means that He is greater than the resurrection of the dead, the salvation from non-existence, and the bestowal of eternal happiness. He is greater than any strange or unimaginable thing, as explicitly stated in the verse: "*Your creation and your resurrection are but as (the creation and resurrection of) a single soul*" (Luqman 31:28).

The resurrection of mankind is as easy for Him as the creation of a single soul. It is in connection with this meaning that, when faced with serious disasters or important undertakings, everyone says: "Allah is the Greatest! Allah is the Greatest!" This phrase is thus made into a source of consolation, strength, and support for mankind.

As is shown in the Ninth Word,[24] the above phrase and its two companions, that is, "Glory be to Allah!" and "All praise be to Allah!" form the nucleus and summary of the daily prayers —the index of all worship— and in order to corroborate the meaning of the prayers, they are repeated while using one's beads following the daily prayers. They provide powerful answers to the questions that arise from the wonderment, pleasure, and awe one feels when faced by the strange, beautiful, and extraordinary things in the universe; these, in turn, cause him to offer thanks and to feel awe at their grandeur. Moreover, at the end of the Sixteenth Word, it is described how at a festival, an ordinary soldier and a field marshal enter the king's presence together; whereas at other times, the soldier can only have contact with the field marshal through his commanding officer. Similarly, in a way resembling that of the saints, a person on the hajj begins to know Allah through His titles of the Lord of All the Worlds and the Earth. With the repetition of this phrase, it is again, "Allah is the Greatest!" that answers all the feverish bewildered questions that overwhelm the spirit as the levels of grandeur unfold in the pilgrim's heart. Furthermore, at the end of the Thirteenth Flash,[25] it is described how it is again the phrase, "Allah is the Greatest!" that answers most effectively

---

[24] See Said Nursi, The Words, The Light, Inc., NJ: 2005.

[25] See, Said Nursi, The Flashes Collection, Sözler Publications, Istanbul: 2000.

Satan's cunning wiles, cutting them down at the root, as well as succinctly, but powerfully answering our questions about the hereafter.

The phrase, "All Praise Be to Allah" also reminds us of the resurrection. It says to us, "I would have no meaning if there were no hereafter. So I say, "To Allah is due all the praise and thanks that have been offered from pre-eternity to post-eternity—whoever has offered them and to whomever they were offered— for the chief of all bounties and the only thing that makes bounty 'genuine bounty,' and saves all conscious creatures from the endless calamities of non-existence, is eternal happiness; it is only eternal happiness that can be equal to that universal meaning.[26]

## The Hajj: A Heavenly Voyage on Earth

The hajj is such a great and comprehensive worship, rendering social unity and intimacy amongst Muslim communities. As the contemporary scholar, Fethullah Gülen, explains, it is impossible to find its profundity or depth anywhere else on earth:

> From the time pilgrims leave their home, they have purified themselves from all the commands and desires of their carnal soul and egotism, and their spirit has become embellished with the silky threads of spiritu-

---

[26] Said Nursi, Şualar, On birinci Şua, Risale-i Nur Collection, Nesil Publications, 967.

al heartstrings. Yes, on this journey, composed of light, humankind meets with the ancient, but never the outmoded; with the earliest, but the eternally freshest truths; and carries out performances and utters expressions that they could never be done or said at any other time. In particular, those who are fully aware of what is happening, with all the memories they gained during the hajj, are uplifted and elevated by this heavenly voyage that takes place on the Earth, with more subtle meanings.

Every year, hundreds and thousands of people feel and breathe their most elusive and delicate thoughts and feelings through the prayers that are performed during the hajj so that they will be able to perform their servanthood to Allah the Almighty with the utmost sincerity, at the summit of all places, at a time when a person can be closest to the Almighty. They all renew their commitment to Allah... And they are purified from all their sins... They remember and remind each other of their responsibilities towards one another... They reconsider all their social, economic, administrative, and governmental affairs, and have another look at them in an environment of worship given to Allah alone, where everything reminds them of their servanthood to the Almighty. At such a time, both their Islamic awareness and consciousness are extremely developed, and they return to their homelands with an expansive new horizon, with a conspicuously new determination, and with an absolutely new enthusiasm.

In a sense, all people go on the hajj with the thought that their souls and feelings have become putrefied. They set off on their journey as if they are entering the world of meanings from a door of which they had never before been aware. On their way, they see and perceive all the principles laid out one-by-one on their path; these are all symbols of Islam. Facing all these signs of Islam, which surprise and enlighten the eyes and hearts, even at the beginning of the journey, they start to be aware of the warm and arousing breeze of the Ka'ba and the excitement of fulfilling the hajj. Then they feel the same pleasant breeze every-where they stop—at bus-stops, on airplane seats, in hotel rooms, in reception halls, and even in the mar-kets and bazaars, until they reach their final destina-tion. This holy journey always bestows one's world of feelings with such a fantastic perception and sen-sation that, in a state of mind that is sometimes over-joyed and sometimes sad, but always self-question-ing and examining, conducted for oneself. Thus, a person always feels alert, as if walking through the corridors of the hereafter.[27]

## The Sanctity of Mecca

In the Qur'an, Mecca is called both "*Al-Balad al-Haram*," The Sacred City, and "*Al-Balad al-Amin*," The Secure City. In relation to the sanctity of Mecca, the Qur'an states:

---

[27] Fethullah Gülen, Yeşeren Düşünceler, 67.

وَقَالُوا إِن نَّتَّبِعِ الْهُدَىٰ مَعَكَ نُتَخَطَّفْ مِنْ أَرْضِنَا ۚ أَوَلَمْ
نُمَكِّن لَّهُمْ حَرَمًا آمِنًا يُجْبَىٰ إِلَيْهِ ثَمَرَاتُ كُلِّ شَيْءٍ رِزْقًا
مِّن لَّدُنَّا وَلَٰكِنَّ أَكْثَرَهُمْ لَا يَعْلَمُونَ

They say: "Should we follow this Guidance in your
company, we would be annihilated in our land." Have
We not established them in a secure sanctuary, to
which, as a provision from Us, products of all kinds
are brought? But most of them do not know (that it is
We Who protect and provide for them, and assume
that it is their worshipping idols that attracts other
Arab tribes to Mecca for trade and that protects them
from being attacked by those tribes). (Al-Qasas 28:57).

All environs of this holy land, called secure and sacred
by Allah, are places where true security and protection
are provided:

لَقَدْ خَلَقْنَا الْإِنسَانَ فِي أَحْسَنِ تَقْوِيمٍ ۞ وَهَٰذَا الْبَلَدِ الْأَمِينِ

And (by) this City secure, surely We have created
human of the best stature as the perfect pattern of
creation. (At-Tin 95:3–4).

The region of the borders of the *Haram*, the Sanctuary, which were defined by the Prophet, have been considered to be places of sanctity since the time of the first
creation. We learn this fact from Safiyya bint Shayba, in
this narration: "I listened to Allah's Messenger in the

year of the Conquest of Mecca. He said: 'O people! Allah has rendered Mecca as *haram* (immune) on the day when He created the heavens and the earth. Here will be *haram* until the Day of Resurrection. Its plants cannot be picked; game animals cannot be frightened; and a lost item can be taken except by someone who announces it to find its owner.' Just at this moment, his uncle, Ibn Abbas said: 'Let the plant of *idhkhar*[28] be excluded from this! For we need this plant for both our houses and graves!' 'Excluding the plant of *idhkhar*!' said the Messenger."[29]

## Mecca, the Unique Mihrab (Direction of Prayer) of Humanity

Apart from some short intervals of time throughout the history of humankind, Mecca has always been the *mihrab*, the niche which indicates the direction one prays in, for humanity. This peculiarity of Mecca is because the Ka'ba is within its borders. In fact, it is the Ka'ba that is actually the niche of humankind. This magnificent *mihrab* also has a *mimbar*, a pulpit, which is called the *Rawda at-Tahira*, the place that is even purer than the Gardens of Paradise.

The Ka'ba is the most sacred place on earth, as declared in the Qur'an:

---

[28] A kind of pleasant smelling herb.
[29] Ibrahim Canan, ibid., no. 6881.

﷼ إِنَّ أَوَّلَ بَيْتٍ وُضِعَ لِلنَّاسِ لَلَّذِي بِبَكَّةَ مُبَارَكًا وَهُدًى لِلْعَالَمِينَ

فِيهِ آيَاتٌ بَيِّنَاتٌ مَّقَامُ إِبْرَاهِيمَ ۖ وَمَن دَخَلَهُ كَانَ آمِنًا

Behold, the first House (of Prayer) established for
humankind is the one at Bakka, a blessed place and a
(center of) guidance for all peoples. In it there are
clear signs (demonstrating that it is a blessed sanctuary, chosen by Allah as the center of guidance), and
the station of Abraham. Whoever enters it is in security (against attack and fear). (Al Imran 3:96–97).

Mecca and the Ka'ba standing in the center of the
*Masjid al-Haram*, the Sacred Mosque, within the city are
both sacred. It is because of the blessings granted upon
this sacred place that so many Prophets have emerged
from here. It can be even stated that, although Prophets
appeared in many parts of the world, the commencement
and origination of nearly all Prophets has been the Ka'ba.
In this respect, this bountiful, sacred place acts like a station for all the Prophets. The supplication of Prophet
Abraham, peace be upon him, must also have an effect on
the Ka'ba, making it a place of security and confidence:

وَإِذْ جَعَلْنَا الْبَيْتَ مَثَابَةً لِّلنَّاسِ وَأَمْنًا وَاتَّخِذُوا مِن مَّقَامِ

إِبْرَاهِيمَ مُصَلًّى ۖ وَعَهِدْنَا إِلَىٰ إِبْرَاهِيمَ وَإِسْمَاعِيلَ أَن طَهِّرَا

بَيْتِيَ لِلطَّائِفِينَ وَالْعَاكِفِينَ وَالرُّكَّعِ السُّجُودِ ﷼ وَإِذْ قَالَ

إِبْرَاهِيمُ رَبِّ اجْعَلْ هَٰذَا بَلَدًا آمِنًا وَارْزُقْ أَهْلَهُ مِنَ الثَّمَرَاتِ

مَنْ آمَنَ مِنْهُم بِاللَّهِ وَالْيَوْمِ الْآخِرِ ۗ قَالَ وَمَن كَفَرَ فَأُمَتِّعُهُ قَلِيلًا
ثُمَّ أَضْطَرُّهُ إِلَىٰ عَذَابِ النَّارِ ۖ وَبِئْسَ الْمَصِيرُ

Remember that We made the House (the Ka'ba in Mecca) a resort for people, and a refuge of safety (a sanctuary, that is, a sign of the truth). Stand in the Prayer (O believers, as you did in earlier times) in the Station of Abraham. And We imposed a duty on Abraham and Ishmael: Purify My House for those who go around it as a rite of worship, and those who abide in devotion, and those who bow and prostrate (in the Prayer). And (remember) once Abraham prayed: "My Lord! Make this (untilled valley) a land of security and provide its people with the produce of earth, such of them as believe in Allah and the Last Day. He (his Lord) answered: "(I will bestow provision upon both the believers and unbelievers. But) whoever is thankless and disbelieves, I will provide for him to enjoy himself for a short while (in this life), then I will compel him to the punishment of the Fire—how evil a destination to arrive at!" (Al-Baqarah 2:125–126).

What is more, despite being situated on a place that is inhospitable for cultivation, neither the people living there nor those who visit there have ever fallen into famine or dire straits, despite the millions of visitors who visit the Ka'ba every year. It has been always a place of a comprehensive peace; and it has mercifully been thus for the last 2,500 years. While violent events occurred in other places, there has always been the blessing of complete security in and around the Ka'ba, at least during the four forbidden months of each year. In 571 CE, the army of Abraha, who had come to Mecca with the intention of demolishing the Ka'ba, was miraculously completely destroyed.

We see that the Messenger gave us the glad tidings that these attributes of the Ka'ba and its surroundings will continue until Judgment Day: "While this community shows the respect to the *Haram* (the Sacred Precincts) that they deserve, the goodness will continue. Whenever they do not act with respect towards them, they will be destroyed."[30]

## Some Places to Visit in Mecca

There are so many places to visit in Mecca. We can list some of these places as follows:

- The blessed house in which our beloved Prophet, the Pride of Humanity, was born, which is situated next to the Masjid al-Haram.
- Mount Hira Nur, where the first revelation was revealed, taking humanity out of the darkness of ignorance into the light.
- The Masjid al-Jinn, built upon the land where some jinn came to the Messenger to declare their

---

[30] Ibrahim Canan, ibid., no. 6882.

submission to him, and where *Sura al-Jinn* was revealed.

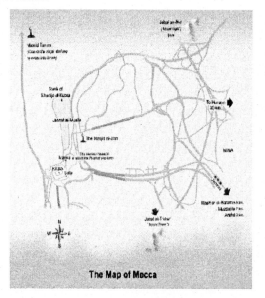

**The Map of Mecca**

- Mount Thawr and the Cave of Thawr; these places were honored by the Messenger and his devoted friend, Abu Bakr, may Allah be pleased with him, for a time when the unbelievers of Mecca tried to prevent them from spreading the light that had been revealed by Allah.
- Jannat al-Mu'alla, the graveyard of Mecca, where Khadija bint Khuwaylid, may Allah be pleased with her, the first beloved wife of the noble Prophet and the first to believe in his message, rests; she sacrificed all her wealth for the sake of his

mission. Also lying here are the grandfather of the Messenger, Abdul Muttalib, many of the Companions, their successors, major scholars, and other righteous people.

## The Ka'ba: A Niche Where the Hearts of Believers Beat Together

The Ka'ba is a niche where the hearts of believers beat together, and it is the only place of worship that has been exalted with the praise of being *"the first House (of Prayer) established for humankind"* on earth. The Ka'ba is a unique building; its sacred past reaches back until Adam and even beyond his creation; it was rebuilt by Prophet Abraham, peace be upon him, after it was ruined and there was no trace of its remains. We are ordered by the Qur'an to remember that long after the flood:

وَإِذْ يَرْفَعُ إِبْرَاهِيمُ الْقَوَاعِدَ مِنَ الْبَيْتِ وَإِسْمَاعِيلُ رَبَّنَا تَقَبَّلْ
رَبَّنَا وَاجْعَلْنَا مُسْلِمَيْنِ ۞ مِنَّا إِنَّكَ أَنتَ السَّمِيعُ الْعَلِيمُ
لَكَ وَمِن ذُرِّيَّتِنَا أُمَّةً مُّسْلِمَةً لَّكَ وَأَرِنَا مَنَاسِكَنَا وَتُبْ عَلَيْنَا
إِنَّكَ أَنتَ التَّوَّابُ الرَّحِيمُ

When Abraham, and Ishmael with him, raised the foundations of the House (they were praying): "Our Lord! Accept (this service) from us. Surely You are the All-Hearing, the All-Knowing. Our Lord! Make us

Muslims, submissive to You, and of our offspring a community Muslim, submissive to You. Show us our rites of worship (including particularly the rites of the Pilgrimage) and accept our repentance (for our inability to worship You as worshipping You requires). Surely You are the One Who accepts repentance and returns it with liberal forgiveness and additional reward, the All-Compassionate." (Al-Baqarah 2:127–128).

As attested in the verse above, Prophet Abraham, the ancestor of Prophets, and his son, Ishmael, rebuilt the Ka'ba upon its original site. Allah the Almighty, Who inspired Abraham to make this supplication, accepted his prayer by sending Muhammad, peace and blessings be upon him, from his generation as the greatest Prophet. When Allah wanted to give, He inspired His servant to request. Upon the profundity and wealth of the Ka'ba, with the spirit of the hajj, nearly everything within the area that surrounds the Ka'ba has gained even more depth and has been given a greater air of magnificence. Circumambulating the Ka'ba and being captivated by its charm, human beings, feeling the pull that is a natural part of their nature, seem to ascend into a helix of light and reach union with their beloved Lord. The circumambulation of the Ka'ba that is performed by a person who has been uplifted to such a spiritual level becomes just like a prostration of thanksgiving; the Zamzam well water they drink becomes just like the water from the

*Kawthar*, The Pond of Abundance in Paradise. It is impossible to show any other place on earth that is more attractive or strikingly effective than the Ka'ba and its surroundings. Those souls that share the good fortune of paying their humble respects to these sacred places are forever saved from the groundless worry of searching for another place to worship.

The Ka'ba is a blessed place that generates a space for genuine peaceful gatherings. While individually performing acts of worship, and thus practicing the religion, every single believer may gain Allah's good pleasure to some extent. However, all rewards gained individually are always defined with limits and conditions. That is, a believer can individually be a recipient of blessings from Allah and enter Paradise. However, the complete and perfect attainment of blessings from Allah can only be obtained through deeds that are fulfilled congregationally. Statements such as, "The hand of Allah is together with those who have congregated" and *"Allah's 'Hand' is over their hands"* (al-Fath 48:10), are very important principles expressing that Divine help, protection, and guidance is with those who have gathered around one aim. On one occasion related to the importance of turning towards the Ka'ba, the great scholar, Said Nursi, said: "I now face the Ka'ba; there are millions of people from all around the world also facing the Ka'ba; and among these millions of people, there are hundreds of benign, saintlike, innocent, and purified individuals." He goes on to explain that, "This line of worshippers amongst which you find yourself forms a circle around the Ka'ba. Another circle is behind this one and also another behind... And these circles continue like this until the final point on the earth. Who knows how many people there are among these lines of people, all of whom are like receptors of Divine secrets, all of whom you are not fit even to hold a candle to." Thus, he elucidates that it is a force holding people together with spiritual ropes. Allah the Almighty has defined it as the point we must face.

## The Ka'ba... A Luminous Column

The following delightful expressions about the Ka'ba are from the heartfelt writings of Fethullah Gülen:

The Ka'ba is like a mother who is seated in the dearest corner, the vantage point of our house, sharing the happiness of her children and grandchildren, and feeling their sorrow deep inside her soul. As she observes all around, she sometimes sheds tears of sadness, and other times, she sends smiles of relief.

When a person starts circumambulating this holiest of buildings, in the holiest of all cities, they feel that they have been warmly embraced by motherly compassion. During the circumambulation, everyone feels light, but secure and happy, just like a child running, yet tightly holding onto his mother's hand. Yes, while pacing around the Ka'ba, as one individual amongst thousands or hundred thousands of people, one is excited with the thoughts of other worlds; one feels emotionally aroused and ecstatic, as if one had ascended towards Allah.

With half of their bodies uncovered and part of their white garments wrapped around their shoulders, the pilgrims are enthused as they stride, with a little haste, but always vigorously and filled with hope.

These are deep souls that are always captivated by the circumambulation of the Ka'ba; during their walk, they pass by countless doors of sanctity... They touch to knock on so many doors of wisdom and raise countless shutters that veil the beyond! It is so exciting that while we walk around this ancient, but never decrepit building, we are truly astonished by the intuitive feelings and the things that we hear which flow into our hearts and minds from all the windows that have been opened in our imagination; we are amazed by the lights that strike our bosoms and we are bewildered by the secrets that make our souls soar. With every step we take forward, we move with a feeling of inspiration that at any moment it will be as if a mysterious gate is opened and we will be suddenly invited inside; we can feel our hearts beating rapidly with excitement.

Although it may be possible to explain all these abstract feelings with some concrete causes, most of the time, we remain quiet before these aspirations and intuitions that are well above the criteria and recognition we possess. This is because, despite external meanings of the material conditions and the external appearance of the Ka'ba and its surroundings, as their true substance is concealed, their core meanings are veiled and the style therein is absolutely Divine; not everyone can comprehend the messages they convey. Nevertheless, there are so many things that all people, no matter their background or education, can understand, though they may not be able to express it in words.

The Ka'ba, nestled amongst many mountains and hills, all of which make us shudder with their grandeur, resembles a water lily that has just unfolded. At the same time it looks like a bell jar which contains the secrets of existence. It is the projection of *Sidrat al-Muntaha*, the Furthest Lote-Tree, upon earth; it is a crystal made up of the essence of the realms beyond.

This is the solid cross-section of a "luminous column" around which innumerable human beings, jinn and angels incessantly circumambulate, from the center of the earth all the way up to *Sidrat al-Muntaha*, the Furthest Lote-Tree. The Ka'ba is a building without peer, and its value is on par with the heavens; billions of pure souls, visible and invisible, long for its sanctuary and seek union therein. In fact, in both the heavens and on the earth, it is called *Baytu'llah*—the House of Allah.[31]

---

[31] Fethullah Gülen, *Yeşeren Düşünceler*, 63-65.

Below, we can read the verse expressing that this is an extraordinarily sacred place described as "My House" by Allah:

وَإِذْ جَعَلْنَا الْبَيْتَ مَثَابَةً لِّلنَّاسِ وَأَمْنًا وَاتَّخِذُوا مِن مَّقَامِ إِبْرَاهِيمَ مُصَلًّى ۖ وَعَهِدْنَا إِلَىٰ إِبْرَاهِيمَ وَإِسْمَاعِيلَ أَن طَهِّرَا بَيْتِيَ لِلطَّائِفِينَ وَالْعَاكِفِينَ وَالرُّكَّعِ السُّجُودِ

Remember that We made the House (the Ka'ba in Mecca) a resort for people, and a refuge of safety (a sanctuary, that is, a sign of the truth). Stand in the Prayer (O believers, as you did in earlier times) in the Station of Abraham. And We imposed a duty on Abraham and Ishmael: Purify My House for those who go around it as a rite of worship, and those who abide in devotion, and those who bow and prostrate (in the Prayer). (Al-Baqarah 2:125).

## A Beaming Staircase That Elevates Us to Other Worlds: The Journey Towards The Ka'ba...

The roads to the Ka'ba are very long and the distances are bitter. They are like the spiritual journey; they are hard trials that purify the soul; they are the surmounting of the difficulties that surround Paradise; they are crossing the ditches of hell. In short, the journey to the Ka'ba entails some distressful trials. Nevertheless, the presence of these difficulties is indispensable as they increase the spiritual stimulation and help lead to the completion of inner preparations. All pilgrims make themselves ready for this journey in accordance to their ability; they are filled to their capacity, and they reach there with a great collection of knowledge and a lofty spirit.

Before, this holy journey used to be performed on horses or camels. In those days, the pilgrims used to visit hundreds of sacred stations and tombs and those of friends of Allah on their way to the Ka'ba. They used to stop at places where the Prophets lived, and they met with them in their imaginations. They used to join in the circles of many sacred and learned scholars and then carry on their journey, illuminated with knowledge as if they were swimming in deep meanings.

Yes, they would travel and finally reach the Ka'ba, with all their ability of deep perception and discernment, triggered by all the things they had seen and heard on this journey; they would see the Ka'ba in all its magnificence, stretching towards the heavens. They would find the Ka'ba examining its visitors from such a height, awaiting them with great hope; and with a strong desire to be united, they would throw themselves into the embrace of the Ka'ba.

All souls that see the outward appearance of this building—which looks like a dignified, light-emitting face, its shadow falling onto the marble floor around it, its meaning that stretches towards and beyond the heavens, and its illuminating atmosphere—begin to hear something from their own dimension, begin to discern the meanings behind this subtle face, and start to taste the happiness that is in the intention of this blessed journey, hidden in a most joyous prayer. They are able to attain the most unattainable of all pleasures...

Those who rush towards the Ka'ba from all corners of the world are carried away by the overwhelming emotion of seeing the Ka'ba before them and, around this common *mihrab*, just like moths flying towards a light; they start searching for a closer interaction with the Real Owner of all the lights. The circumambulation of brave men seems to be conducted around the Ka'ba; in reality, however, this circumambulation is performed in an infinite environment within a helix of light based upon heartfelt intuition.

With all its meaning, spirit, essence, and values in the eyes of human beings, the Ka'ba becomes like a scholar who reads poems, admonishes, encourages, or teaches its followers. The Ka'ba is also like the one who initiates and leads the circle of the remembrance of Allah in the middle of the stone piles, hills and hillocks all around it. The Ka'ba is like the inner sanctum, open to intimate friends; and its surroundings are like the reception hall, open to strangers; the hills of Safa and Marwa are like observatories for observing the heavens of truths; the Station of Abraham is like a luminous staircase elevating us to worlds beyond; and the well of Zamzam is like a cupbearer in this passionate meeting. Greeted by these sacred sites all at once, the travelers of love attain an other-worldly presence and start observing the Divine dominion; the human imagination sets sail for such a vast horizon that the travelers feel as if they were to take one more step, they would enter the wondrous realm of the beyond.

Although the Ka'ba is an earthly building, and it is built from materials collected from its environment, it gives the impression of a water lily that has rooted and blossomed in the heavens and which carries all the mysteries of existence in its soul; we can sense, although indirectly, that the Ka'ba has connections with both the earth and the heavens. It is the most dignified, the noblest and the most historical jewel which carries signs from all periods of the past, and it is an ancient construction that has remained, with its value ever-increasing with each passing day. Just as Adam, peace be upon him, was the most significant source for the spirits, characters, and attributes of all generations that descended from him, so too is the Ka'ba the mysterious home that contains the spirit, meaning, and substance for all constructions and buildings on earth.

Every duty and obligation performed around the Ka'ba has a charm particular only to these obligations, and it is impossible for believing hearts to remain indifferent to the effect of this charm. Souls who turn around the Ka'ba and turn into an immense flood with their ever-increasing number, with the fascination and excitement they feel in the midst of this cascade, completely forget everything related to themselves and wake up in a completely different inward and spiritual world. They feel that their most personal and sincerest love and desires are expressed with every word, with every adoration, and with every plea offered in this sacred place; they witness that their innermost heartfelt feelings are vocalized in the most mystical words and with the feelings commingled with the sound, light, and harmony that exists here; and they gain an everlasting memory of the most unattainable happiness.[32]

## The Ka'ba: The Radiant Connection Between the Earth and the Heavens

The Ka'ba is not merely a building made of stones; it is also a radiant link that connects the earth to the heavens... During the *Miraj* (the Ascension) of our Prophet, nothing but this luminous column, which stretches to the heavens from the earth to the *Sidrat al-Muntaha*,[33] dazzled the eyes of our beloved Prophet.

---

[32] See Fethullah Gülen, Zamanin Altin Dilimi, 187-190.

[33] Literally, the Sidrat al-Muntaha is the Lote-tree of the furthest limit, signifying the boundary between the realm of Divinity and the realm of creation.

In addition, the angels are constantly circumambulating this wonderful array of bright colors; they are so great a host that when one angel completes its circumambulation, it cannot have another turn around the Ka'ba. In this respect, the Ka'ba is the projection of the *Sidrat al-Muntaha* upon the earth, reaching into its inner core. Whatever the *Sidrat al-Muntaha* is in the world of meanings, the Ka'ba is the same for the material world, and it is as if it is the cornerstone of all things that exist.

## The Place from Whence Divine Revelation Poured Down

The universal messages of the universal religion first began to be revealed in this blessed place. Divine Revelations pour down upon some certain places and, in this regard, the Ka'ba has an outstanding characteristic—that is, it is a connection between the earth and the heavens. While looking upon the human community, the Prophethood, and the capability of humankind to represent the Prophethood, it is as if Allah the Almighty looks through the axis of the *Sidrat al-Muntaha*, the heavens, and the Ka'ba. In this regard, as the Qur'an is the linchpin of the earth, and it is thanks to the Holy Qur'an that everything is laid out before us; if everything on earth remains standing today, this is because of the Ka'ba. Maybe because of this, Our Prophet said that the destruction of the Ka'ba would be one of the most important signs of the Day of Judgment. For the destruction of the Ka'ba would mean that there would no longer be any faith or religion on the earth, and there would be no reason for the earth to survive anymore.

## The Circumambulation of the Ka'ba Is Like Prayer

Allah's Messenger declared that, "The circumambulation of the House is like the prayer, except that you can speak while you perform this. Therefore, whoever speaks during the circumambulation, let him speak only of what is good and beneficial."[34] In this regard, he also said, "Speak little during the circumambulation of the Ka'ba, for you are, then, in the prayer."[35]

Abdullah ibn Abbas, may Allah be pleased with him, reports: "Allah's Messenger said, 'Those who makes fifty circumambulations of the House (the Ka'ba) will be purified from all their sins and become as pure as the day they were born.'"[36]

There are narrations that say that sitting in a corner and watching the Ka'ba when one is exhausted from circumambulating the Ka'ba is a rewarding form of worship. Ja'far ibn Muhammad, may Allah be pleased with him,

---

[34] Tirmidhi, Hajj, 112, no: 960; Nasai, Hajj, 136, 5/222.

[35] Nasai, Hajj, 136, 5/222.

[36] Ibn Jawzi, Ilal al-Mutanahiya, 2/574.

narrates from his father who reported from his grandfather that Allah's Messenger said, "To look at the House (the Ka'ba) is worship." In another hadith narrated by Abdullah ibn Abbas, may Allah be pleased with him, Allah's Messenger, peace and blessings be upon him, said, "Looking at the Ka'ba is pure faith." Sa'id ibn al-Musayyab, may Allah be pleased with him, narrates the following hadith about this subject: "A person who looks at the Ka'ba with complete faith and approval of its value will be purified from all their sins, as pure as they were on the day they were born."[37]

## The Sa'y (Striding) Between the Hills of Safa and Marwa

The Prophet said the following about the ritual of striding between the hills of Safa and Marwa: "Circumambulating the *Baytu'llah*, striding between Safa and Marwa, and stoning Satan are commanded for the remembrance of Allah."[38] Circumambulating the Ka'ba is a form of worship and remembrance of Allah; the striding between Safa and Marwa is also a route that has been determined for us to concentrate solely upon remembering Allah. The hills of Safa and Marwa are sacred places where we offer our sincere prayers and present our requests, par-

---

[37] Ibn Adiyy, Al-Kamil fiy Duafai ar-Rical, 6/101.

[38] Abu Dawud, Manasik, 51, 1888; Tirmidhi, Hajj, 64, 902.

ticularly those for prosperity in the hereafter, and where we express our weakness, poverty, and desperation to All-Powerful Allah, just as our blessed mother, Hagar, did hundreds of years ago.

## Supplications While Striding Between Safa and Marwa

The route of this ritual is also a place of worship. As we have learned all the other prayers that are performed during the hajj from our blessed Prophet, we also learn what to do here from him as well. Abdullah ibn Saib, may Allah be pleased with him, narrates: "I heard Allah's Messenger saying this prayer while he was striding between Safa and Marwa: 'O Our Lord! Give us what is good in this world and give us what is good in the hereafter, and save us from the torment of the hellfire.'"[39]

Nafi' Mawla ibn Umar says that Abdullah ibn Umar, may Allah be pleased with him, was saying this prayer on Safa: "O My Allah, You say in the Divine Book 'Call on Me, I will answer you.' Surely, You are the One Who keeps His words, and I request from You now: You guided me and blessed me with Islam, so please do not take it away from me. Grant me to give my last breath as a true Muslim."[40] O our All Compassionate Lord! We implore

---

[39] Abu Dawud, Manasik, 52, 1892.
[40] Malik, ibid., 128.

that You may accept the invocation expressed by Abdullah ibn Umar also for us!

Ibn Umar, may Allah be pleased with him, used to say, "Allah is the greatest!" three times, and then used to utter the following: "There is no deity but Allah; He is One; He has no partner; the rule and possessions of all belong to Him; all thanks and praise that have been expressed and will be expressed all belong to Him; He is the Most Powerful over everything." And he used to repeat this seven times. He used to repeat the same statements also on Marwa."[41] In one narration from Razin ibn Sulayman al-Ahmari, it is said that: "This makes twenty-one *takbir* of "*Allahu akbar*" (Allah is the greatest!), and seven *tahlil* of "*La ilaha illa'llah*" (There is no deity but Allah). Between these readings, he used to pray, imploring and calling on Allah, and then he would start to come down the hill. When he reached the green pillars at the bottom of the valley, he would start running and then continue to run until he emerged from this part; when he reached the side of Marwa, he used to carry on walking. When he had climbed to the peak of the hill, he used to stand there for a while and then he used to repeat the same prayers he had recited on Safa. He used to repeat this seven times and, thus, complete his worship."

---

[41]  Malik, Muwatta, Hajj, 127.

# Incessant Effort to Find What One Is Looking For

In expressions of sufism, if we think of circumambulating the Ka'ba being like '*sayr fi'llah*,' or spiritual journeying 'in' Allah—which denotes a voyage that begins around a very auspicious feeling and  thought, with an aim of gaining more depth within our own souls—then rushing backwards and forwards between Safa and Marwa can be regarded as '*sayr ila'llah*,' or journeying towards Allah and '*sayr mina'llah*,' or journeying 'from' Allah, which denotes the ascension from creation towards the Creator, and descending from the Creator towards the creation. Yes, in the movement backwards and forwards between Safa and Marwa, one can have such a high, sublime experience and such a deep flow of feelings and senses emerging from it.

In the rhythm of their striding back and forth between these two hills, and under the storm of such feelings, the pilgrims experience the running in search of aid, the entreaty for relief, and the crying out for a helping hand. There, successive pursuits continue, as if in pursuit of something very crucial. These comings and goings will continue until the thing that is sought appears. With every sign and every mark that one encounters on the way, one's excitement increases...

And in the same way that it happens around the Ka'ba, where one both runs and explores their inner soul, gaining self-depth, here, between the hills of Safa and Marwa, with Prophet-like feelings and sensations, one rushes forwards and backwards in a straight line, rushing but controlled, worried but hopeful, smiling and crying for others. Under the golden lights of the heavens, carrying the excitement of a new reunion, while also having sadness at not having been able to find exactly what one is seeking, one moves forwards and backwards—running and walking slowly, climbing up the hill and coming—and one struggles through the wavering that may happen on one's own personal journey.

During this ritual, one is sometimes with others, joining in the murmurings of the river of running people, vocalizing one's own feelings within this chorus; and one sometimes feels as if one sees no one and nobody, as if one is performing this worship alone, visualizing Hagar, awaiting the mercy that will extinguish all the fires inside... And together with the fire that burns one's own soul, one is parched with the never-ending yearning for journeying towards the Beloved.

In the place where this ritual is performed, realities are mixed with dreams, and people all around are seen sometimes in the deepest silence, and sometimes expressing screams and laments. Pilgrims experience both worry and pleasure; it is as if they have drifted towards the "mizan" (the scales in which the deeds of everyone shall be weighed), sometimes as if they are running towards the *Kawthar* pond in Paradise, and sometimes at ease... They continue to move forwards and backwards, climbing up and down.[42]

## Mecca Revived and Re-Inhabited

Prophet Abraham, peace be upon him, received the command from his Lord to take Hagar and Ishmael to Mecca years before he was ordered to rebuild the Ka'ba. In obedience to the order of his Lord, Prophet Abraham was to leave his baby son, Ishmael, and his wife, Hagar, on a bare desert land where there was neither vegetation nor water. He took Hagar and Ishmael to a place which showed no trace of prior habitation. Although it was to be a place which would be the most honored place on earth centuries later; he left them there and went back to his home. While doing this, Prophet Abraham, peace be upon him, was actually demonstrating what a sincerely loyal person should do. Allah had commanded him to take his wife and his son to Mecca, a place that would become the cradle for many civilizations, and settle them there. As due a person who is an intimate friend of Allah, Abraham's loyalty and submission were tested through the most strenuous trials. And still, many more difficult tests that were hard to bear awaited him.

---

[42] Fethullah Gülen, *Yeşeren Düşünceler*, 67.

Despite his great love and affection for his wife and baby son, Prophet Abraham returned to the land of Canaan without looking behind him at all. Most probably this was because he feared that if he were to look back, he would not be able to obey the order of his Lord, and perhaps the weeping of his wife would be unbearable, causing the close relation between himself and his Lord to be destroyed. After he had gone on about three hundred or five hundred meters, he heard his wife, Hagar, shouting: "O Abraham! O Abraham! Are you doing this because it is the command of Allah, or is it your own decision?" Hagar asked such a question as she was a faithful servant of Allah and had grasped the true cause behind this event. This action showed the generations that would follow centuries later just how worthy she was to be the ancestor of the Blessed Last Messenger of Allah.

Faced with such a question, Prophet Abraham, peace be upon him, gathered all his strength and found the opportunity to tell Hagar the truth behind all that had happened and said that: "By the command of Allah, and only by the command of Allah, have I left you here." Upon this reply, Hagar said, "As you brought and left us here by the command of Allah, then I know that Allah will not abandon us, nor leave us wretched and lost."

While bearing all these hardships, Hagar acted with tranquility, as she submitted herself fully to Allah's will, in obedience to all His orders, knowing with conviction that He would never abandon her in this difficult situation. Because of this characteristic, she is seen as an inspiring woman of strength, vision, and insight. Her behavior exhibited exemplary behavior for all coming generations. This exemplary behavior was adopted by other people over time, and the path blazed by them has become a wide road on which many blessed individuals have proceeded. Generations with devoted hearts who walk on this road are still following these reverent guides (Prophet Abraham and Hagar) in order to feel anew the things that they experienced as part of their original pilgrimage.

## Hagar Runs Frantically Between the Hills of Safa and Marwa

Prophet Abraham, the Intimate Friend of the All-Compassionate Lord, was returning to the land of Canaan in peace and confidence. Ishmael, the initial light of the lights that continue until Doomsday, the honored ancestor of Prophet Muhammad, the Pride of Humanity, peace and blessings be upon him, was only a little baby in swaddling. He did not have anybody to protect him other than his mother, Hagar. After a while, the food and drink that had been given to Hagar were finished. There was no water, nor any food for them, in this uncultivable valley. The only thing visible was some vultures circling in anticipation of their death. But there was no need for worry or fear! Vultures are also under the command of Allah!

After Prophet Abraham, peace be upon him, had left, the entire load was upon Hagar. But she said: "If it is the command of Allah, then I have nothing to worry about at all"... After a little while, the baby started to cry because he was very thirsty. He was crying incessantly. Not being able to bear seeing her son suffer, Hagar started running frantically, trying to find some water. The first place she ran to was the hill of Safa. She climbed to the peak of this hill. The whole while, she pleaded: "Will I be able to see any water anywhere? Or will I see any birds that indicate the existence of water? I am not important, but this tiny baby is crying for water, and this is saddening for me..." The mother acted out of a strong feeling of affection, according to the laws established by Allah. Perhaps all this was for the sake of the Last Prophet, who would come from her progeny.

When she could see nothing from Safa, she ran a distance of about four hundred meters and climbed up the hill of Marwa. Then, she heard Ishmael crying and ran back to him. Then she again ran back up to Safa, looked around and then desperately ran back up to Marwa. She ran backwards and forwards seven times. She ran to Safa four times and came to Marwa three times. From that day on, running between these two hills became a ritual prayer, reminding us of our own despair. The area in which one runs is called the *mas'a* (running place), and this worship is called *sa'y*.

Having found nothing, despite running backwards and forwards, Hagar collapsed and pleaded: "Oh my Lord! I am in desperate straits. I have done everything I can. I have tried everything I can think of. What will I do now? I cannot leave this tiny innocent baby of mine and go away, neither I can act in opposition to what You have commanded. I cannot rebel against my husband... He told me to stay here! I am finished now, I am in despair. My darling son is crying because he is so thirsty. You can see his situation. I am also extremely tired and desperate. You also know my situation..." In His Infinite Mercy, Allah responded to her earnest supplication, as He listens to those who invoke to Him:

أَمَّن يُجِيبُ الْمُضْطَرَّ إِذَا دَعَاهُ وَيَكْشِفُ السُّوءَ وَيَجْعَلُكُمْ خُلَفَاءَ الْأَرْضِ ۗ أَإِلَٰهٌ مَّعَ اللَّهِ ۚ قَلِيلًا مَّا تَذَكَّرُونَ

*"Who answers the helpless one in distress when he prays to Him, and removes the affliction from him, and makes you vicegerents of the earth? Is there another deity besides Allah? How little you reflect!" (an-Naml 27:62).*

Just at the moment when all causes become hopeless, just at the point where the candle has burnt out to the end, and just at the place where all worldly assistance ceases, there is a refreshing, reviving breath from the Divine World:

> At the place you never expect,
> An all-encompassing curtain is opened,
> A cure for that affliction is attained,
> Let us see what our Lord will arrange,
> Whatever He arranges,
> He does it in the best manner.
>
> (İbrahim Hakkı of Erzurum)

The plea of Hagar, who was in desperate straits, was answered, as water surged out where the baby's feet were kicking. This is the water that has flowed since that day, which is known as the Well of Zamzam. Millions of pilgrims drink this water, use it and carry it to their homes in numerous containers... This is the Zamzam water that splashed and flowed between the feet of Ishmael and which turned the bare desert land into gardens of paradise, vivifying and giving new life to Mecca...

Having done all what was supposed to have been done when one is in difficulties, and having put all her trust in Allah, Hagar found the Zamzam right by Ishmael. She tried every way that might enable her to find a solution, and when all the possibilities were finished, she put herself in Allah's hands and did what any devout believer should do. And Allah, miraculously, took all her worries away and made her happy at the most unexpected moment. Not only did He make her happy, but with the favor He granted Hagar, Allah the Almighty also made all of humankind happy. Thus, He turned Mecca, which was once a desolate desert land into a highly respected, prestigious place. Allah the Almighty added honor upon honor to the Ka'ba; the angels themselves make continuous circumambulations around it up to the *Bayt al-Mamur* (the House over the heavens parallel to the Ka'ba at Mecca).

Only Allah knows for certain, but perhaps Zamzam is a re-emergence that has been sent forth in honor of the Ka'ba. Allah, Who erected the Ka'ba before, also created the Well of Zamzam during the time of Prophet Adam, peace be upon him. Ishmael's foot hitting there was only an external cause for Zamzam to be rediscovered. According to this perspective, in time, as Allah's instructions and prohibitions began to be neglected and Meccans no longer listened to Divine commands, perhaps the water of Zamzam dried up and its location was no longer apparent. Such "forgetfulness" or neglect may happen in cycles, then. For as Zamzam was somehow forgotten between Prophets Adam and Abraham, again, sometime between that momentous event whereby Hagar and Ishmael "rediscovered" Zamzam until the time of Abdul Muttalib, the grandfather of Prophet Muhammad, peace and blessings be upon him, the location of the Well of Zamzam also became obscured. According to some narrations, when the time for the Messenger approached, Allah the Almighty showed a sign to Abdul Muttalib, the grandfather of Prophet Muhammad, peace and blessings be upon him, suggesting to him in his dream that he dig at the present-day location of the Zamzam well. Upon awakening from this dream, Abdul Muttalib dug the waterhole and excavated Zamzam; both the people of Mecca and the pilgrims who come to Mecca now continue to use it and drink from it.[43]

## The Water of Zamzam to Drink With Great Enjoyment

Muhammad ibn Abdur Rahman ibn Abu Bakr, may Allah be pleased with him, narrates: "I was sitting by Ibn Abbas. One man came over to us. 'Where are you coming from?' he asked. 'From the Well of Zamzam!' the man answered. Upon this, Ibn Abbas asked: 'Did you drink from it in the required manner?' When the man asked what the required manner was, he explained: 'When you are drinking the water of Zamzam, you must turn yourself towards the *qibla*. Say *Bismillahir Rahman-ir Rahim*. Drink it in three gulps, breathing at each. When you finish, you will express your thanks to Allah. For Our Blessed Prophet ordered that: 'The difference between us and hypocrites is that the hypocrites do not relish drinking from Zamzam."[44]

---

[43] Abdur Rahman Suhayli, Ar-Rawd al-Unf, II, 95.

[44] Ibrahim Canan, Hadis Ansiklopedisi, no. 6871.

## Drinking the Zamzam Water for Whatever One Intends

Jabir ibn 'Abdullah, may Allah be pleased with him, narrates: "Allah's Messenger announced: 'The Zamzam is beneficial for whatever aim it has been drunk for.'"[45]

Abdullah ibn Abbas, may Allah be pleased with him, narrates: "I offered the Zamzam water to Allah's Messenger, and he drunk it while standing."[46]

Abdullah ibn Umar, may Allah be pleased with him, narrates: "At the time of the Treaty of Hudaybiya, Allah's Messenger asked one Qurayshi man to bring Zamzam water to Hudaybiya. The man brought it, and Allah's Messenger took it to Medina."[47]

Our beloved Prophet once came to the Zamzam well. The children of Ibn Abbas, may Allah be pleased with him, were drawing water from the well and were distributing it to the pilgrims. The Messenger complimented them, saying, "Continue to draw the water! You are performing a good deed." Then he continued: "If I did not think that people would flock in from all quarters, I would dismount from my camel and even put the rope of the

---

[45] Ibrahim Canan, ibid., no. 6872.

[46] Bukhari, Hajj, 76, Ashriba 16; Muslim, Ashriba, 117, 2027; Tirmidhi, Ashriba, 12, 1883.

[47] Ibrahim Canan, ibid., no. 1541.

well here (pointing to his shoulder with his hand), and I would draw the water, just like you."[48]

As we can see from all these narrations, Zamzam water is regarded as sacred in the religion of Islam. It satisfies the hunger of the person who drinks it even when he or she is actually hungry; it quenches the thirst of a person who drinks it when he or she is thirsty; and it becomes a means of healing for a person who drinks it with the intention of gaining recovery from an illness. All believers who

The Zamzam water in the white opaline bottles sealed with red wax Topkapı Palace Museum, Inventory no. 21/763

The practice of consuming the Zamzam water to treat ill people or to break the fast can be traced back to the time of the Prophet's Companions. It is recorded that a mantle of the Prophet had been handed down by Aisha to her sister Asma, who used to give the ill the Zamzam water left from a washing of the mantle of the Prophet.

---

[48] Zabidi, Tecrid-i Sarih Tercemesi, (Tajrid as-Sarih, trns.), 6, 126.

come to Mecca from all around the world for the hajj or umra carry back bottles and bottles full of the Zamzam water to their countries and offer it to their friends and visitors.

## A Night in Mina on the Eve of the Day of Arafat

While performing the Farewell Hajj, one day, before climbing the Mount of Mercy in the valley of Arafat, our Blessed Prophet spent a day and night in Mina and, with this, taught us to spiritually prepare ourselves for standing at Arafat. "During this hajj, on the eighth day of Dhu al-Hijja, that is the day before the Eve of the Eid, Allah's Messenger performed the Noon, Afternoon, Evening, and Night Prayers as well as the Morning Prayer of the Day of Arafat, in Mina."[49]

## Mina Waits for Its Guests

With its incredible spirituality and amazing magnetism, Mina awaits the pilgrims at a place on the route leading to Arafat, where the creaking of the gates of the heavens can be heard... Muzdalifa seems that it will not let them go before granting them the experience of a small *Shab'i Arus*, a time for union and meeting with the Beloved. Further on, pilgrims will come to a place where they will announce their complete obedience and submission to

---

[49] Ibrahim Canan, ibid., no. 6862.

Allah and stone the mentality which has no worry but the worldly struggle of making a living; they will offer the ransom of their own souls and taste the great pleasure of salvation in their own personal worlds. Then in the Ka'ba, they will turn towards the real Ka'ba of their hearts, and conclude their ascent and descent from The Ultimate Truth again to The Ultimate Truth. With the knowledge they have gained through *'fana fi'llah,'* self-annihilation in Allah, and *'baqa bi'llah,'* subsistence with Allah, they will present all their thanksgivings to their Lord Who has bestowed all these experiences on them.

Being positioned at a place of pure altruism and self-lessness, with its charming array of notable attributes, Mina makes its utmost harmony heard on the hills of Muzdalifa. The effect of Mina is to make pilgrims want to enter Muzdalifa, then to surpass Muzdalifa, and to salute Arafat, that is even greater and just beyond. Thus, it warmly greets all its guests, becomes a point of reference for them, and then conveys and entrusts these precious guests to Arafat itself.[50]

## The Hajj Is Arafat

After Allah's Messenger performed the Morning Prayer on the day before the 'Eid of Sacrifice, he moved towards the plain of Arafat and reached there at noon.

---

[50] Fethullah Gülen, Yeşeren Düşünceler, 68.

While Allah's Messenger was on the *Jabal ar-Rah-ma*, the Mount of Mercy in the valley of Arafat, he told those with strong voices to repeat these words so that everyone could hear: "The hajj is Arafat; whoever reaches the standing at Arafat before the time for the Morning Prayer on the night of Jam' (that is, gathering before dawn at Muzdalifa), will have fulfilled the (requirements of the) hajj."[51] Allah's Messenger himself stood at Arafat until sunset, with the pilgrims accompanying him, and then they left there for Muzdalifa. As pointed out in the hadith above, those who do not reach the area of Arafat until sunset need to stand at Arafat before the dawn of 'Eid, as those who reach the dawn of the 'Eid Day without having stood at Arafat will have missed the hajj.

We can find the following verses in the Qur'an which are related to Arafat and Muzdalifa:

لَيْسَ عَلَيْكُمْ جُنَاحٌ أَن تَبْتَغُوا فَضْلًا مِّن رَّبِّكُمْ ۚ فَإِذَا أَفَضْتُم مِّنْ عَرَفَاتٍ فَاذْكُرُوا اللَّهَ عِندَ الْمَشْعَرِ الْحَرَامِ ۖ وَاذْكُرُوهُ كَمَا هَدَاكُمْ وَإِن كُنتُم مِّن قَبْلِهِ لَمِنَ الضَّالِّينَ

There is no blame on you that you should seek the bounty of your Lord (by trading during the Hajj, but beware of preoccupation to the extent of neglecting

---

[51] Tirmidhi, Hajj, 57, 889; Abu Dawud, Manasik, 69, 1949; Nasai, Hajj, 211, 5/264; Ibn Maja, Manasik, 37, 3015.

any of the rites of the Hajj). When you press on in multitude from Arafat (after you have stayed there for some time,) mention Allah at Mash'ar al-Haram (al-Muzdalifa); mention Him, being aware of how He has guided you, for formerly you were surely of those astray. (Al-Baqarah 2:198).

As for the sequence of the hajj rites, after the standing at Arafat on the day before the 'Eid Day, after sunset, the pilgrims proceed to Muzdalifa. The *Mash'ar al-Haram*, the place where we are told "*mention Allah at Mash'ar al-Haram*," is in Muzdalifa. Evening and Night Prayers are jointly performed in Muzdalifa. Pilgrims spend the night there, and on the first day of 'Eid, after the Morning Prayer, they move towards Mina.

According to a narration from Aisha, may Allah be pleased with her, Allah's Messenger said: "It is on the Day of Arafat (i.e. the day before 'Eid) that Allah frees His servants the most from the hellfire."[52]

## Arafat: A Glorious Day Spent Amidst the Angels

Yes, the hajj is Arafat, and the standing at Arafat is the central rite. Blessings that will be attained during this stay in the Valley of Arafat are much more valuable than any that can be earned in an entire lifetime. It may be

---

[52] Muslim, Hajj, 436; Nasai, Manasik, 194; Ibn Maja, Manasik, 56.

only a day, but it is a day full of acquisitions that are worth a lifetime.

Arafat has such a luminance, and the time spent there has such depth, that a fortunate spirit who has had the opportunity to be in such a holy atmosphere, even if it was only once, can never completely deteriorate and will never pass away as a soul bound to the world. Those who spend only a few hours of their lives on Arafat will always open up and bloom like roses, all through the rest of their lives, and they will never fully fade. There, minutes satiated with compassion, love, and poetic rhythms always glitter in the eyes of our hearts, just like the sunshine... And everywhere, we hear the cries of people who have become tender through their revealed or veiled sacred love, and who trill like nightingales as they express aloud their faith, their Divine knowledge, and their earnest love; all of these are engaged in a detailed network in the innermost and hidden parts of their hearts. They are eager to reach the other worlds and beyond, and their souls enthusiastic for the next stage.

For the human soul to become more uplifted and subtle, then, it should, at least once in its lifetime, find itself in the atmosphere of Arafat; it must at least once taste the experience of Arafat, and it should fully inhale atmosphere of Arafat, to be raised and lowered, to begin and end. While we are making both our physical and metaphysical preparations for lifting our souls in Mina, at the same time, Arafat is being adorned from one end to the other, and is

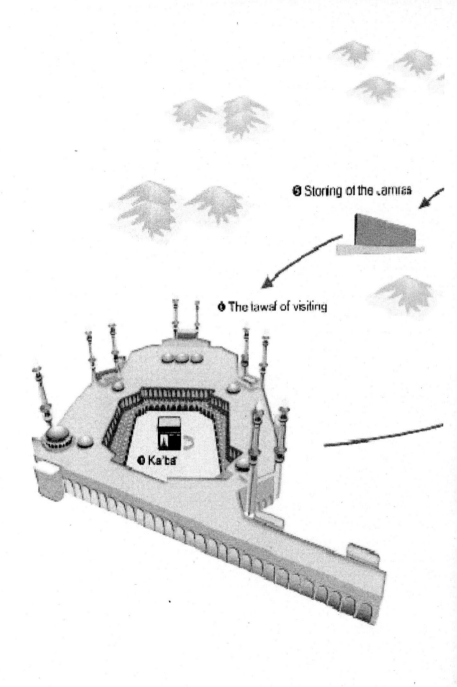

❺ Storing of the ḥamras

❻ The ṭawaf of visiting

❶ Ka'ba

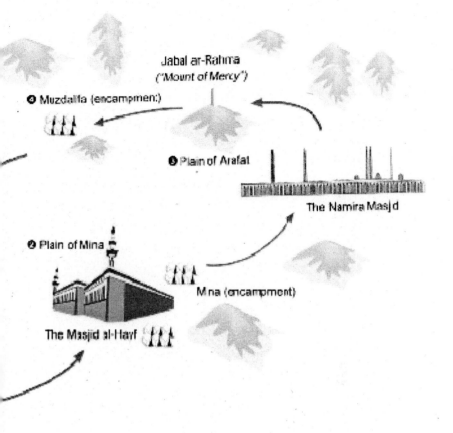

Jabal ar-Rahma
("Mount of Mercy")

❹ Muzdalifa (encampment)

❺ Plain of Arafat

The Namira Masjid

❷ Plain of Mina

Mina (encampment)

The Masjid al-Hayf

**The route the pilgrims take during the hajj**

preparing its bosom, like a harbor, a square, or a ramp; it begins to wait for Allah's guests who will come and land on it, who will stretch out towards the other worlds, and who will run towards it with a deep feeling of longing.

Arafat is a place of mercy and blessing where human beings always walk amongst groups of angels; where individuals always surrender to sublime and lofty feelings and thoughts; where the Mercy of Allah pours down upon our hearts; and where events incite hope in us. Arafat is a square of judgment where individuals experience the anxious suspense of being questioned for their every deed. Human beings who have been removed from everything that belongs to the worldly life walk on the plains of Arafat, feeling both the uneasiness of the reckoning in the Hereafter and the hope of being forgiven by the All-Compassionate Lord. They expect to be granted forgiveness for all the sins they have committed throughout their lives and hope that they will be of those who are saved; on that one day in Arafat, they try to attain a reward and spiritual advantage which can only be gained through many years of prayers, sincere repentance, and asking for forgiveness.

## Arafat Is the Place of Imploring

Arafat is the place where one implores and adores. On Arafat one witnesses the most sincere, the most hair-raising, the most inciting adorations and pleas. Particularly towards the afternoon, when the time of departure is approaching, the prayers which are expressed in a more emotional spiritual mode are felt much deeper; the voices and breaths at that time reach such an immense level of profundity and lucidity that they greatly resemble the laments of angels in the heavens beyond. As one hears the laments and weeping that arises from the plains of Arafat—the spirituality of these sounds, and their tenderness, affection, and trust, which are rendered in the hope of attaining eternal prosperity—one feels as if one has become younger, that one has been eternalized, and as if one has entered through a great opening and thus grown greater. Particularly at the time when the sun sets and the horizon darkens, releasing the mist of farewell, we feel as if all hopes have been crystallized and poured into us, as if our conscience has become illuminated with what we have gained from Arafat; just like in a dream, it is as if we have emerged from our bodies and are sailing towards some metaphysical world... we feel that we are lamenting and wailing like Arafat itself... that we have also melted away, together with the setting sun... that we also have become a cry, just like those laments that echo in our ears... we have become lighter and somehow are flying like birds... It is as if we have changed our nature and been transformed into some metaphysical form. In the amazement and astonishment in which we find ourselves, we remain where we are standing.[53]

## Moving to Muzdalifa En Masse from Arafat

On the Eve of the 'Eid Day, the Quraishi people, who could not digest the command of fulfilling the duties at Arafat, the most important principle of the hajj, returned to Muzdalifa, objecting: "We are the original dwellers of the Ka'ba; that is, we are privileged people who live just by the Ka'ba. We do not want not to leave the Grand Mosque for the *wuquf* (standing) and will not go to Arafat; we can perform our *wuquf* (standing) in Muzdalifa, separately from those who come from the provinces." Upon this, the following verse was revealed:

ثُمَّ أَفِيضُوا مِنْ حَيْثُ أَفَاضَ النَّاسُ وَاسْتَغْفِرُوا اللَّهَ

Then (do not choose to remain in Muzdalifa without climbing Arafat so that you will not mix with other people because of vanity. Instead,) press on in multitude from where all the (other) people press on. (Al-Baqarah 2:199).

## The Standing in Muzdalifa

In Muzdalifa, the holy place where pardon is granted, Allah's Messenger expressed these words to the people

---

[53] Fethullah Gülen, Yeşeren Düşünceler, 61.

on the morning of their standing in Muzdalifa: "In this Muzdalifa, Allah the Almighty bestowed upon you bene-faction and favor and forgave the sinners for the sake of those who have done good deeds among you. He grant-ed the decent and good ones whatever they wanted. There-fore, move from here to Mina in the Name of Allah!"[54]

## "What Has Made You Smile, O Allah's Messenger?"

Abbas ibn Mirdas, may Allah be pleased with him, nar-rates: "During the Farewell Hajj, on the evening of the day before the 'Eid, Allah's Messenger implored Allah so that his community be forgiven. Allah the Almighty replied to his prayer: "I have forgiven all of your commu-nity, except for those who have acted atrociously. I will take revenge for the aggrieved upon the atrocious." Allah's Messenger implored: "O Lord! If you wish, as a bounty from Your Presence, You can grant from Paradise for those who are oppressed and forgive those who are atrocious!" However, Allah did not reply to him that night. Allah's Messenger performed the Morning Prayer in Muzdalifa and repeated his prayer that had as yet received no reply the night before and his prayer was then answered as he wished. Out of gratification and joy, Allah's Messenger smiled. When Abu Bakr and Umar, may Allah be pleased with them, said: "May my mother and father be sacrificed

---

[54] Ibn Maja, 56; Ahmad ibn Hanbal, 4/14-15.

for you, O Allah's Messenger! You have never smiled so much at this time of the day. What has made you smile? May Allah make you happy all the time!" Allah's Messenger replied: "When Iblis, the enemy of Allah, learnt that Allah granted pardon to all of my community, he took the earth from the ground and scattered it all around his face and started to yell and shout out, 'Woe unto me! I have completely perished! All of my efforts have come to nothing!' To see this fear and sadness on his part made me smile."[55]

The expression, "O Lord! If You wish, You can grant from Paradise for those who are oppressed!" in the above hadith means that the Prophet asked for forgiveness for the unjust behavior of Muslims, and that all that is desired be given to the Muslim who has been faced with an unjust act. He also desired that those who had been unjust be forgiven from Allah's bounty. It is difficult to say whether Our Prophet made this prayer first in Arafat and then in Muzdalifa for all of his community, with no regard to whether they had gone on the hajj or not; or just for the part of his community that had gone on the hajj; or perhaps only for his Companions who had joined him on the hajj. If we consider this hadith as being glad tidings of, "being purified from all sins just as on the day they were born," for those who perform a hajj graced with

---

[55] Ibrahim Canan, ibid., no. 6863.

Divine acceptance and pleasure, then we can interpret this as glad tidings for all who have gone on the hajj.[56] Allah knows best.

## Muzdalifa: The Blessed Place Where Salvation Is Granted

On the way back from Arafat, as soon as we receive the message that Muzdalifa is waiting for us, we leave the lights that surrounded us and leave Arafat, that place that has smiled on us so promisingly, and we walk towards Muzdalifa; this is regarded as a place of closeness to Allah, similar to the closeness of the prostration in the prayer, and compared to the closeness obtained during the bowing in humility during the prayer. We walk towards Muzdalifa, just as we walk towards eternity, infinity, and towards the presence of Allah. There, in a very blessed place where the light of the nearly full moon flutters over the hills and streams, valleys and slopes, carrying us with heavenly and uplifting feelings, although our feet are on the earth, we find ourselves at an eminent pier, a different harbor, a distinguished ramp that leads us to Allah the Almighty. With our states unchanged since being at the Ka'ba, we see the reflections of the heavens on the faces of the pilgrims; we hear the sincerely imploring

---

[56] See Haydar Hatipoğlu, Sünen-i Ibn Mace Tercemesi ve Şerhi, (Annotated Interpretation of Ibn Maja's Sunan), 8/262.

voices of devoted servants who are completely turned towards Allah, forgetting all else; we feel only the sensitivity in our hearts; and we walk there as if we were walking around the gardens of other worlds.

Ibn Abbas, may Allah be pleased with him, tells us that Prophet Muhammad, the Pride of Humanity, peace and blessings be upon him, received in Muzdalifa the spiritual acquittal for his community which he could not openly receive in Arafat. How I wish that this determination of Ibn Abbas, may Allah be pleased with him, was a hundred percent right! If it is as Ibn Abbas says, then Muzdalifa, the place that draws us close to Allah to the degree that sincere prostration in the prayer does, requires that we express earnest and heartfelt pleading, beseeching, praying, and imploring.

All around Muzdalifa, the gleaming lights, along with the pilgrims with tearful eyes, bright faces, and fast-beating hearts, create a mesmerizing and stupendous beauty that embraces this sacred piece of land which we know only for one night. Particularly in the smaller hours of the night, every inch is covered with even deeper veils of secrets. While some people take rest to be prepared to fulfill their strenuous duty the following day, others spend their night in prayers and supplications until the morning.

Those individuals who listen to their hearts, speak with their hearts, and live beyond the limits of time, living with melodies that are vocalized by their hearts, hear in a great chorus all the chants and tuneful sounds that they have tried to play on the strings of their hearts, with the plectrum of their feelings and sensations, erupting in Muzdalifa this day. As signs of dawn appear on the horizon, the meaningful sounds and breaths that were felt just a day ago on Arafat pour into Muzdalifa with ever-increasing excitement and emotions. They pour in, and the first light of day breaks with many emotions and many sounds of laments. When not in the prayer, pilgrims turn their souls towards Allah; and when in prayer, they want to be only and solely with Allah. Further, as another dimension of closeness to Allah, each of the supplications that flow into their prayers, like the special *qunud* prayers which are said in the last part of the last prayer of the day, are told with such depth and sensibility that they can never properly be described.

Sometimes, like a silk garment, they cover us and nurture our feelings. Sometimes, like heavenly hands, they invigorate our hopes and console our sorrows. Sometimes, like the call to prayer, they announce the highest truth and send thrills inside our hearts. And sometimes, bringing all the pieces of our scattered world together, they make us feel and hear such meanings from our essence, our infinity, our world, and our hereafter that it feels as if we are rediscovering ourselves, meeting our essence more closely, waking up to the world from a different perspective, and seeing the other world from a nearer and clearer viewpoint.

The pleas and laments in Muzdalifa continue until the moment that the sunlight appears with the glad tidings of a new day on the horizon. And, when the sun rises, the pilgrims, who have effectively been continuously in prostration to their Lord until that very moment, start setting off to achieve a different sort of intimacy with their Creator.[57]

## Rejoining Mina After Arafat

Now, in front of us is Mina, where we stopped before and where we left our greetings in its valleys. Mina is the place where crystallized hearts encompass the simple logic and hand it over to the soul. Mina is the place where souls that have fully submitted themselves display their sincere devotion. And Mina is where thousands and hundreds of thousands of people, from the time of Prophet Adam to Prophet Abraham, and from him to Allah's Messenger, the Glorious Star of the Humanity, have restrained their personal logic and intellect, rather connecting their reasoning and senses to their hearts. Finally, in addition to all these spiritual experiences, Mina is the place where our ego gets its own share of subjugation while we are stoning Satan; what is more, Mina is

---

[57] Fethullah Gülen, ibid., 63.

the place where forms of worship are congregationally performed without the usual search for wisdom or necessity—for they are performed merely because they have been ordered by Allah.

Apart from stoning Satan, there are many other things performed in Mina. These include the sacrifice of a sheep, cow, goat, or camel; shaving the head and beard for men; removing the *ihram* that had been worn since the time when the intention for fulfilling the hajj was first made; and the compulsory circumambulation of the Ka'ba, which is performed with the complete metaphysical alertness that has been gained through one's concentration being intensified by the journey here.[58]

## Mina: The Place Where Subtlety in Obedience to the Divine Order Is Felt

I think Mina is like a warm embrace in a celestial atmosphere, a place where selflessness comes together with compassion, where we comprehend the subtlety of obeying the Divine Command with love and affection. Mina is like a hive of submission and a home for volunteers. Mina is such a mysterious and compassionate place that nearly every homeless, dispossessed person can settle for a few days. In earlier times, this was completely true; but now, unfortunately, it is only partially true, due to the

---

[58] Fethullah Gülen, ibid., 64.

large number of pilgrims. In this sacred stopover, situated amongst mountains and valleys, every heart that is not completely closed to the other worlds can feel and sense so many special emotions!

We find Mina merged so much into our souls that we feel as if Mina is beating in our hearts. It is such a feeling that as soon as we step into Mina, we sense that it embraces our souls, just as it opened its bosom first for the Messenger of Allah. We feel that it points us along the paths that lead to different worlds and thus, we all become, in a way, like Mina itself.

## Remember Allah in Those Numbered Days!

فَإِذَا قَضَيْتُم مَّنَاسِكَكُمْ فَاذْكُرُوا اللّهَ كَذِكْرِكُمْ آبَاءَكُمْ أَوْ أَشَدَّ ذِكْرًا فَمِنَ النَّاسِ مَن يَقُولُ رَبَّنَا آتِنَا فِي الدُّنْيَا وَمَا لَهُ فِي الْآخِرَةِ مِنْ خَلَاقٍ

And when you have performed those rites, mention Allah as you mentioned your fathers (with the merits you approve of in them), or yet more intensely. (Al-Baqarah 2:200).

In the time before the revelation, the Arabs used to gather together in Mina after having completed the hajj and feel proud, becoming puffed up by praise, and boasting about the deeds of their ancestors. The following verse, however, encourages remembering Allah, under-standing His guidance, comprehending and thinking over His creations. It commands us to thank and praise His endless bounties instead:

وَاذْكُرُوا اللّٰهَ فِي أَيَّامٍ مَّعْدُودَاتٍ فَمَن تَعَجَّلَ فِي يَوْمَيْنِ فَلَا إِثْمَ عَلَيْهِ وَمَن تَأَخَّرَ فَلَا إِثْمَ عَلَيْهِ لِمَنِ اتَّقَىٰ وَاتَّقُوا اللّٰهَ وَاعْلَمُوا أَنَّكُمْ إِلَيْهِ تُحْشَرُونَ

Mention Allah during the (three) appointed (num-bered) days (of 'Eid of Sacrifice) (with *takbirs*). Who-ever is in haste and content with two days (of men-tioning Allah, having performed the rite of stoning Satan), it is no sin for him; and whoever delays (con-tinuing the rite to the third day), it is no sin for him, for him who is careful of the bounds of piety. Keep from disobedience to Allah in due reverence for Him and piety, and know that you will be gathered to Him. (Al-Baqarah 2:203).

Related to these verses, in his commentary on the Qur'an, Ahmet Hamdi Yazir gives us this information: "In particular, remember Allah by saying "*Allahu Akbar!*" on the numbered days which are called the *tashriq* days, during which after every compulsory prayer, we must utter this phrase. In the verses that mention the hajj, the phrases 'numbered days' and 'known days' are used. 'Known days' are explained as the first ten days of the month of *Dhu al-Hijja* or the *ayyam an-nahir* (that is, the tenth, eleventh and the twelfth days of *Dhu al-Hijja*) and by common consent, 'the numbered days' are explained as the *ayyam at-tashriq* (that is, the eleventh, twelfth and the thirteenth days of *Dhu al-Hijja*). *Tashriq* means saying "*Allahu Akbar, Allahu Akbar, La ilaha illa'llahu Allahu Akbar, Allahu Akbar wa Li'llahil Hamd*," out loud. This special phrase, which is called *tashriq takbir*, and which is uttered aloud, is connected to Prophet Abraham, peace be upon him. The days from the dawn of the Eve of the 'Eid of Sacrifice until the evening of the fourth day of 'Eid are the days of *takbir* and remembrance of Allah, and 'the numbered days' can be any of these five days.

However, the first of these days is the Eve (*Arafat Day*), three of them are the days of sacrificing, and the fifth is only a day of *tashriq*. The phrase the 'days of *tashriq*,' however, is related to the eleventh, twelfth and thirteenth days of *Dhu al-Hijja* in particular—that is, the second, third, and fourth days of the 'Eid—and these days are those on which stoning is performed in Mina with loud *takbirs*. In this respect, although the days of *takbir* are five altogether, since the day before the 'Eid and the first day of the Eid are included in the 'known days,' 'the numbered days' must then be these three *tashriq* days. The Qur'anic statement, "*Whoever is in haste and content with two days (of mentioning Allah, having performed the rite of stoning Satan),*" also confirms this. By performing the

122

rite of throwing pebbles at Satan and uttering *takbirs*, the pilgrims acknowledge and declare that Allah is infinitely and absolutely great, and there can be none comparable with Him. According to narrations, on these days, Umar, may Allah be pleased with him, used to read *takbirs*, and so did those around him, as did even those who were on the roads and who were in *tawaf*. In short, it means that the verse mentioned above, "*Mention Allah as you mentioned your fathers*," defines the actual remembrance that one must be engaged in all the time; while the order, "*Mention Allah during the appointed (numbered) days*," commands us a special remembrance to be fulfilled with *tashriq takbirs*. Apart from the known remembrance on the day before the 'Eid and on the 'Eid Day itself, after each of your prayers and while performing the stoning, reflect and announce the Greatness of Allah by uttering *takbirs* out loud on the three *tashriq* days. In this case, whoever hastens to return to their homeland and finish their hajj duties in two days, to set off on their journey back, there is no blame on them."[59]

## The Place Where the Qur'anic Chapter of al-Baqarah Was Revealed

Abdur Rahman ibn Zayd, may Allah be pleased with him, narrates: "Ibn Mas'ud stoned Satan by throwing seven

---

[59] Elmalili Ahmet Hamdi Yazir, Hak Dini Kur'an Dili, II/62-63.

~ 123 ~

pebbles at the bottom of the valley at the place to stone Satan. With each stone, he uttered *Allahu Akbar*, "Allah is the greatest!" loudly. At that moment, he was standing with the Ka'ba on his left and Mina on his right side. When he was told, 'People are throwing their stones from above!' he replied, 'I swear to the One apart from Whom there is no other god that this is the post where *Sura al-Baqarah* was revealed."[60]

---

[60] Bukhari, Hajj, 135-138; Muslim, Hajj, 305, 1296; Tirmidhi, Hajj, 64, 901; Abu Dawud, Manasik, 78, 1974; Nasai, Hajj, 226, 5/273.

# Chapter 3

# The Major and Minor Pilgrimages
# of the Messenger

## The Hajj and Umra of Our Beloved Messenger

As for all other acts of worship, it is very important for the believers to learn the exact practices of the Messenger and follow how he performed the rites of hajj. About performing the prayers, our Prophet suggested: "Look at me and perform your prayers as I perform," and his community tried to follow this. Performance of the prayers, as Allah's Messenger taught them, has reached us today without any change. And as is the case for the prayers, Muslims have tried, and are still trying, to perform the rites of hajj worship in just the same way that Allah's Messenger practiced these in terms of what, where and how; for some Companions of the Blessed Prophet followed every step of the Messenger and recorded all of his prayers in detail, providing us with a clear explanation of which worship was performed where.

In the following narration, Abdullah ibn Abbas, may Allah be pleased with him, explains how Prophet Muhammad, peace and blessings be upon him, performed the hajj: "Allah's Messenger left Medina for the purpose of fulfilling the hajj duty. When he came to the Masjid Dhu al-Hulayfa, which is ten kilometers away from Medina, he actually started the hajj worship by praying there two rak'ats of *salat al-ihram* (the prayer performed after a pilgrim changes into the apparel of hajj). After he completed the prayer, he recited the *talbiya* for hajj. Some people heard this *talbiya* prayer. I also heard this from him and memorized it. Then he mounted on his camel, and when the camel stood up, he again recited the *talbiya*. Some people heard this *talbiya* as well. I also heard this from him and I kept it in my mind. Then he mounted on his camel. When his camel stood up, he re-recited the *talbiya*. There were also some people who heard this second *talbiya*. It was because the people were scattered and were in constant movement that, each time, different people heard his *talbiya* prayers. Thus, his second *talbiya* that he recited when his camel lifted him up was heard by some new people. They were these people who said: 'Allah's Messenger recited *talbiya* when his camel lifted him up.' Allah's Messenger carried along on his way. When he reached the Hill of Baydha, he again recited *tal-*

biya. There were some other people here who heard this talbiya of Allah's Messenger. These people said: 'Allah's Messenger recited talbiya when he reached the top of Baydha.' By Allah, Allah's Messenger recited talbiya as soon as he prayed the two rak'ats of salat al-ihram in the mosque in Dhu al-Hulayfa and made his intention for the hajj and started the hajj prayer. Then when he mounted on his camel he recited another talbiya, and when he climbed up the Baydha Hill, he recited another talbiya there."[61]

Abdullah ibn Umar, may Allah be pleased with him, used to stop reciting talbiya when he reached the closest place to the Haram region. Then he used to pass the night at a place called Dhu-Tuwa, perform Morning Prayer there, then take ghusl, the ritual bath, and say that: 'This is how Allah's Messenger also did it.'"[62]

Ibn Umar, may Allah be pleased with him, narrates: "Allah's Messenger performed an umra, or minor pilgrimage until the hajj and offered a sacrificial animal. He had brought his sacrificial animal with him all the way from Dhu al-Hulayfa. He started to perform all the umra rites, by making intention for performing umra, and then recited the talbiya for umra. Then he made his intention for the hajj and recited the talbiya for hajj. All of his Com-

---

[61]  Abu Dawud, Manasik, 21, 1770.
[62]  Bukhari, Hajj, 39-39; Muslim, Hajj, 226, 1259; Muwatta, Hajj, 32, 1/333.

panions accompanying him also did umra until the hajj. There were some people among the pilgrims bringing their own sacrificial animals with them, and some without a sacrificial animal. When he reached Mecca, Allah's Messenger spoke these words in public, (whose source can be found in the Qur'an itself, in the 196th verse of Surah al-Baqarah): *"Whoever has got a sacrificial animal, let him not come out of his ihram until the whole hajj is completed; whoever has not got any sacrificial animal with him, let him perform his tawaf and sa'y and shorten his hair and then come out of the ihram. Then let him put on his ihram again for hajj and sacrifice his animal; let him who cannot find a sacrificial animal fast for a total of ten days—for three days during the hajj, and for seven days when he has returned to his home.'"*[63]

Ikrima, may Allah be pleased with him, narrates: "Ibn Abbas was once asked about *hajj tamattu*, combining the hajj and umra with a break in between. He replied as follows: 'During the Farewell Hajj, the Emigrants, the Helpers, and the wives of Allah's Messenger all donned *ihram* clothes, so did we. When we reached Mecca, Allah's Messenger ordered: 'Apart from those who have brought an animal for sacrifice, let everybody change their *ihram* worn for the hajj into the intention of umra.' Upon this

---

[63] Bukhari, Hajj, 104; Muslim, Hajj, 174, 1227; Abu Dawud, Hajj, 24, 1805; Nasai, Hajj, 50, 5, 151-2.

command, we circumambulated the *Baytu'llah*. We strode between Safa and Marwa. Then we came out of our *ihrams*, joined our wives, and dressed up our daily garments. Allah's Messenger has also said this: 'Whoever has an animal for sacrifice, let him not come out of *ihram* until his animal reaches the sacrificial place!' In the evening of *Tarwiya* (the eighth day of Dhu al-Hijja, or the day before the eve of the 'Eid), Allah's Messenger ordered us to don our *ihrams* for the hajj. Upon this, we went out the region of Haram, donned our *ihrams*, started performing our hajj; and, after completing the rites, we returned Mecca, circumambulated the *Baytu'llah*, and performed *sa'y* between Safa and Marwa. Thus we completed our hajj worship, as stated in the Qur'an:

وَأَتِمُّوا الْحَجَّ وَالْعُمْرَةَ لِلَّهِ ۚ فَإِنْ أُحْصِرْتُمْ فَمَا اسْتَيْسَرَ مِنَ الْهَدْيِ

"*Complete the Hajj and the umra for Allah, and if you are impeded (after you have already put on the Pilgrimage attire), then send (to Mecca) a sacrificial offering you can afford...*" (al-Baqarah 2:196). So then we sacrificed our animals."[64]

"While he was saluting the Hajar al-Aswad during umra, Allah's Messenger used to stop reciting the *talbiya*."[65]

*Talbiya* recited by Allah's Messenger was composed of these words: "*Labbayk Allahumma labbayk, Labbayk la*

---

[64] Bukhari, Hajj, 37.

[65] Tirmidhi, Hajj, 79, 919.

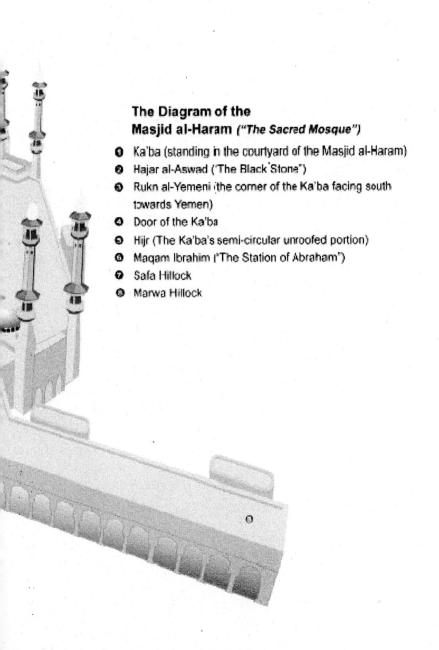

## The Diagram of the
## Masjid al-Haram *("The Sacred Mosque")*

❶ Ka'ba (standing in the courtyard of the Masjid al-Haram)

❷ Hajar al-Aswad ('The Black Stone")

❸ Rukn al-Yemeni (the corner of the Ka'ba facing south towards Yemen)

❹ Door of the Ka'ba

❺ Hijr (The Ka'ba's semi-circular unroofed portion)

❻ Maqam Ibrahim ('The Station of Abraham")

❼ Safa Hillock

❽ Marwa Hillock

*sharika laka labbayk, Inna'l-hamda, wa'n-ni'mata laka wa'l-mulk, La sharika lak.*" ("Here I am, O Allah, at Your command! Here I am at Your command! You are without associate! Here I am at Your command! Yours are praise, grace and dominion! You are without associate.") He did not add any other word to this supplication.[66]

## The Messenger's Entry to Mecca and the Ka'ba

"Allah's Messenger performed the *ghusl*, or ritual bathing, before he entered into Mecca."[67]

Aisha, may Allah be pleased with her, narrates: "I strongly desired to enter the Ka'ba and pray inside it. Allah's Messenger held my hand and took me inside the Hijr (the unroofed portion of the Ka'ba in the form of a semi-circular compound towards the north of the Ka'ba), and told me, 'If you want to enter the Ka'ba, perform your prayer here. For here is a part from Ka'ba. While your tribe was reconstructing the Ka'ba for the purpose of restoring it, they shortened the size of Ka'ba from its original size and kept this part (the Hijr) outside the building of the *Baytu'llah.*'"[68]

---

[66] Bukhari, Hajj, 26; Libas, 89; Muslim, Hajj, 19, 1184; Muwatta, Hajj, 28, 1, 331-332; Tirmidhi, Hajj, 13, 825; Abu Dawud, Manasik, 27, 1812; Nasai, Hajj, 54, 5, 159-160.

[67] Tirmidhi, Hajj, 29, 852.

[68] Tirmidhi, Hajj, 48, 876; Abu Dawud, Manasik, 94, 2028; Nasai, Hajj, 129, 5, 219.

## The Messenger's Circumambulation of the Ka'ba

"Allah's Messenger came to Mecca. He straightaway entered the Masjid al-Haram and greeted the Black Stone. Then, keeping the Ka'ba on his left, he walked briskly during the first three rounds of tawaf, and he walked at a normal pace during the last four circles around the Ka'ba. Then he came to the Station of Abraham and read the 125th verse of Sura al-Baqarah:

وَإِذْ جَعَلْنَا الْبَيْتَ مَثَابَةً لِّلنَّاسِ وَأَمْنًا
وَاتَّخِذُوا مِن مَّقَامِ إِبْرَاهِيمَ مُصَلًّى

"*Remember that We made the House a resort for people and a refuge of safety (a sanctuary, that is, a sign of the truth). Stand in the Prayer (O believers, as you did in earlier times) in the Station of Abraham...*" After this, standing between the Station of Abraham and the Ka'ba, he prayed two rak'ats of prayer. When he completed his prayer, he again came by the Hajar al-Aswad and saluted it. Then he strode between Safa and Marwa. I think he read there the 158th verse of Sura al-Baqarah:

إِنَّ الصَّفَا وَالْمَرْوَةَ مِن شَعَائِرِ اللهِ ۖ فَمَنْ حَجَّ الْبَيْتَ أَوِ اعْتَمَرَ فَلَا
جُنَاحَ عَلَيْهِ أَن يَطَّوَّفَ بِهِمَا ۚ وَمَن تَطَوَّعَ خَيْرًا فَإِنَّ اللهَ شَاكِرٌ عَلِيمٌ

"*(The hills of) Safa and Marwa are among the emblems appointed (to represent Islam and the Muslim community).*

*Hence whoever does the Hajj to the House (of Allah, i.e., the Ka'ba) or the umra, there is no blame on him to run between them (and let them run after they go round the Ka'ba as an obligatory rite). And whoever does a good deed voluntarily (such as an additional circumambulation around the Ka'ba, running between Safa and Marwa, and other kinds of good actions), surely Allah is All-Responsive to thankfulness, All-Knowing."*[69]

In another narration from Abu Dawud, it is stated that "When Allah's Messenger came to Mecca, he was ill. Because of this, he performed his circumambulations mounted on his camel. During the *tawaf*, each time, he came in front of the *rukn* (*rukn al-Yemeni*, or the corner of the Ka'ba facing south towards Yemen), he saluted it with his stick. When he completed his *tawaf*, he dismounted from his camel and performed two *rak'ats* of prayer."[70]

## The Polytheists' Intention of Tantalizing Muslims

Ibn Abbas, may Allah be pleased with him, narrates: "When Allah's Messenger and his Companions came to Mecca, they were feeling fatigue because of yellow fever, which they had caught in Yathrib (the former name of Medina). Polytheists spread around the city certain gos-

---

[69] Muslim, Hajj, 147/1218, 235/1263; Muwatta, Hajj, 107, 4, 364; Tirmidhi, Hajj, 33/856, 34/857; Nasai, Hajj, 149, 5, 228; Ibn Maja, Manasik, 29, 2951.

[70] Abu Dawud, Manasik, 49, 1881.

sip claiming: 'Tomorrow will come a group of people whose energy and strength have run out and who are worn out because of yellow fever,' and they sat behind the Hijr and waited there to tantalize the Muslims. Upon learning about this mischief of the polytheists through Divine revelation, in order to show the polytheists that he and his followers were strong and inviolable, Allah's Messenger ordered the Muslims to make *raml* (walking briskly, accompanied by movements of the arms and legs to show one's physical strength) during the first three rounds of *tawaf*, and walk at a normal pace between the two corners. Seeing this scene, the polytheists said: 'Are these the people whom you thought felt weak due to yellow fever? They are even stronger than such-and-such people!' Ibn Abbas, may Allah be pleased with him, stated that: "What prevented Allah's Messenger from commanding his Companions to run during all of the rounds of the *tawaf* was nothing other than his compassion towards them.'"[71]

## These People Are Like Gazelles

Allah's Messenger removed the upper piece of his *ihram* from his right shoulder (by passing it under the right armpit to place it on the left shoulder), saluted the Hajar

---

[71] Bukhari, Hajj, 55; Maghazi, 43; Muslim, Hajj, 240 1266; Tirmidhi, Hajj, 39, 863.

al-Aswad, recited words of *takbir*, and then performed three rounds of brisk walking. When Muslims came by the *Rukn al-Yemeni*, the corner of the Ka'ba which faces Yemen, when they were concealed from the sight of the people of Quraysh, they walked at a normal pace; but when they became visible to the Qurayshi people, they walked briskly again. Seeing Muslims walking so vividly and gracefully, the Qurayshi people said to each other, "These people are just like gazelles."[72]

In a narration reported in Bukhari and Muslim, it is stated that: "Allah's Messenger conducted three rounds of brisk walking from Hajar al-Aswad back to Hajar al-Aswad, and walked (at a normal pace) for four more rounds; after he completed his circumambulations of the Ka'ba, he performed two rak'ats of prayer. Then, he strode between Safa and Marwa during both umra and the hajj." Ibn Umar, may Allah be pleased with him, narrates: "Allah's Messenger never ceased to salute the Hajar al-Aswad and the *Rukn al-Yemeni* on each circumambulation of the Ka'ba."[73] And, "During the two rak'ats of the prayer performed after completing the circumambulations, Allah's Messenger recited *Sura al-Kafirun* and *Sura al-Ikhlas*."[74]

---

[72] Abu Dawud, Manasik, 51, 1889.

[73] Abu Dawud, Manasik, 48, 1876; Nasai, Hajj, 156, 5, 231.

[74] Tirmidhi, Hajj, 43, 869.

## Striding Between Safa and Marwa

Ibn Umar, may Allah be pleased with him, was asked: "Did you see Allah's Messenger speeding up his pace between Safa and Marwa? Ibn Umar, may Allah be pleased with him, answered: "Yes. He was together with a group of people. They were speeding up their pace altogether. I saw people around him speeding up to the same tempo as Allah's Messenger, peace and blessings be upon him."[75]

## Proceeding First to Mina Then to Arafat

Ibn Umar, may Allah be pleased with him, narrates: "Allah's Messenger, after performing the Morning Prayer in the morning of Arafat Day (the eve of the 'Eid), set off from Mina to Arafat and reached Namira. Namira is the place where the supervisors who come to Arafat gather. When it was noon time, Allah's Messenger moved from Namira under the intense heat. He combined the noon and afternoon prayers together, and he performed both of these prayers one after the other. He then gave a speech to the people. Then he walked and stopped at a place on Arafat for the *wuquf* (the standing at Arafat)."[76]

---

[75] Nasai, Hajj, 175, 5, 242.

[76] Abu Dawud, Manasik, 60, 1913.

## The Standing at Arafat

Abdurrahman ibn Ya'mur, may Allah be pleased with him, narrates: "While he was on Arafat, Allah's Messenger ordered the public crier to announce these words: 'The hajj is Arafat. Whoever can reach the standing at Arafat before the dawn after the night of Jam' (Muzdalifa), it means he performed the prayer of the hajj. Stoning satan in Mina is three days. Whoever will hurry to perform this in two days, there is no blame upon him; and there is no blame, either, upon the person who would like to extend it.'"[77]

Ali, may Allah be pleased with him, narrates: "Allah's Messenger stood up for the *wuquf* on Arafat and he said: 'Here is Arafat, here is the place for the *wuquf*. Everywhere on Arafat is a place of *wuquf*.' Then, as soon as the sun set, he hastened to leave Arafat (for Muzdalifa). He was riding his camel together with Usama ibn Zayd. While people all around his left and right sides were excitedly trying to spur their camels, without facing towards them, he remained calm, as was his usual mood at all times, calling, 'O people! Calm down,' which he was also saying and expressing with a hand gesture."

---

[77] Tirmidhi, Hajj, 57, 889, Abu Dawud, Manasik, 69, 1949; Nasai, Hajj, 211, 5, 264; Ibn Maja, Manasik, 37, 3015.

## Leaving Arafat

Then the Prophet came to Jam' (Muzdalifa). He led the evening and night prayers jointly. When morning broke, he came to the Hill of Kuzah and stood for *wuquf*. "'Here is Kuzah—it is a place of *wuquf*. Everywhere on Jam' is a place of *wuquf*,' he said. Then he left there and came to the valley of Mukhassir, where he spurred his camel so that the camel galloped through the valley. He stopped over there and mounted Fadl, the son of his uncle Abbas, may Allah be pleased with him, on his camel. From there he came to the *Jamra al-'Aqaba* (a stone pillar), the largest of the three *jamras* (pillars), and threw pebbles at the *Jamra al-'Aqaba*. After this, he came to the place of sacrificing and said: 'This is the place where we will sacrifice our animals; everywhere on Mina is a place for slaughtering sacrificial animals.'

"A young woman from Has'am tribe came and asked him: 'O Allah's Messenger! My father is an old man upon whom the hajj has become compulsory. May I perform the hajj on his behalf?' Allah's Messenger replied: 'Perform the hajj on your father's behalf!' At that moment, he bent Fadl's head down with his blessed hand. Upon this, his uncle, Abbas, asked: 'O Allah's Messenger! Why did you bend your cousin Fadl's head down?' Allah's Messenger replied: 'I can see that both of them are young. I am not sure about the evil (whisperings) of satan against them!'

"Then a man came and exclaimed: 'O Allah's Messenger! I performed the *tawaf al-ifadha* (the circumambulation around the Ka'ba that the pilgrims must perform after coming from Mina to Mecca on the 10th of Dhu al-Hijja) before I shaved!' Allah's Messenger answered: 'You can now shave; there is no objection to this!' Then another man came and cried out: 'O Allah's Messenger! I unfortunately conducted the sacrifice before I performed the stoning!' Allah's Messenger answered: 'You can now throw your pebbles; there is no objection to this.'

"Then Allah's Messenger came to the *Baytu'llah*, performed his circumambulations, and then came by the Well of Zamzam and said: 'O Children of Abdul Muttalib, if I did not have the concern of people flocking in from all quarters, I would also go down the well and draw water from the Well of Zamzam.'"[78]

In another narration related by Usama ibn Zayd, this event is explained as follows: 'When the sun set, Allah's Messenger hastened to leave Arafat. When he came to the mountain pass, he dismounted his camel and went to answer nature's call. Then he took ablution. While taking his ablution, he used only a little amount of water, not a great amount. 'Will we perform the prayer, O Allah's Messenger?' I asked then. He replied: 'No, the prayer is awaiting ahead us!' and mounted on his camel. When he came to Muzdalifa, he dismounted his camel

---

[78] Tirmidhi, Hajj, 54, 885.

and took ablution again. This time he used more water. Then the prayer began as he performed the evening prayer. Then everybody made their camels crouch. Then, again, prayer started, but this time, he performed the night prayer. He did not perform any other prayer in between these two prayers."[79]

## Talbiya Recited on Arafat and Muzdalifa

Muhammad ibn Abi Bakr as-Saqafi, may Allah be pleased with him, narrates: "While coming to Mina from Arafat, I asked Anas ibn Malik about talbiya: 'How were you conducting it while you were with Allah's Messenger?' He replied as follows: 'People who desired to say talbiya were reciting this; Allah's Messenger was not interfering with this. And whoever wanted to say tahlil said tahlil; Allah's Messenger was not interfering with this, either. None of us would blame his friend just because he was saying different dhikrs (invocations)."[80]

Abdurrahman ibn Muadh, may Allah be pleased with him, narrates: "While we were in Mina, Allah's Messenger addressed us. Our ears became so alert to his words that whatever he was saying, we could very comfortably

---

[79] Bukhari, Wudu, 6, 35; Hajj, 93,95; Muslim, Hajj, 266, 1280; Muwatta, Hajj, 19, 1, 400-401; Abu Dawud, Manasik, 64, 1925; Nasai; Mawakit, 56, 1, 292; Hajj, 206, 5, 259.

[80] Bukhari, Hajj, 86; 'Eidayn, 12; Muslim, Hajj, 274, 1285; Nasai, Hajj, 192; 5, 250.

hear all of his words from where we were. In a moment, he began to explain about the prayers for the hajj. He explained everything up to the part relating to the stoning place. Then he put his fore and middle fingers on his ears while he was speaking. He explained that the stones to be thrown should be no bigger than chick peas. He ordered the Emigrants to settle at the front part of the mosque, and the Helpers to settle at the back of the mosque. Only after this did everybody dismount from their camels and settle down for the night."[81]

Again, Aisha, may Allah be pleased with her, narrates: "On the night before the 'Eid, Allah's Messenger sent Umm Salama to Mina. Umm Salama completed throwing pebbles before the break of dawn. Then she went and conducted her *tawaf al-ifadha*."[82]

## "Could You Pick Up Stones for Me?"

Ibn Abbas, may Allah be pleased with him, narrates: "On the morning of the stoning (of the stone-built pillars, or *jamras* of) Aqaba, while he was still on his mount, Allah's Messenger asked: 'Could you pick up stones for me?' I picked up small pebbles that are just big enough to be thrown with forefinger and thumb. When I put the pebbles on his palm, he said, 'There! Like these ones; do not

---

[81]  Abu Dawud, Manasik, 70, 1951; Nasai, Hajj, 189, 5, 249.

[82]  Abu Dawud, Manasik, 66, 1942; Nasai, Hajj, 223, 5, 272.

deviate to exaggeration in religion. Those before you were destroyed by their exaggeration in religion!'"[83]

## The Prophet Came Back to Mina

Anas ibn Malik, may Allah be pleased with him, narrates: "Allah's Messenger came to the *Jamra al-Aqaba*, the largest of the three *jamras*, threw his pebbles, and then came to the place where he settled in Mina and offered his sacrifice. Then, pointing the right side of his head, he told the barber, 'Cut from here!' Then he pointed to the left side of his head, and he started to give his hairs to the people around (who were looking forward to getting his blessed hair). He gave the hair cut from his right side to the people who were on his right, and he gave the hair cut from his left side to the people who were on his left. In another narration, it is said that: He gave the hair cut from his left side to Abu Talha and ordered him to, 'Give these out to the people!'"[84]

## "Perhaps I Will Not Be Able to Perform the Hajj Again With You"

Jabir ibn Abdullah, may Allah be pleased with him, narrates: "On the day of the 'Eid of Sacrifice, I saw Allah's

---

[83] Nasai, Hajj, 217, 5, 268.

[84] Bukhari, Wudu, 33, Muslim, Hajj, 323, 1305; Tirmidhi, Hajj, 73, 912; Abu Dawud, Manasik, 79, 1981.

Messenger throwing pebbles while riding his camel. He threw his pebbles while he was mounted on his camel and said this: 'Learn your rituals from me. I do not know—maybe I will not be able to perform any other hajj after this year.'"[85]

Ibn Umar, may Allah be pleased with him, saw the blessed Prophet on another occasion walking to the *jamra* to throw pebbles: "Allah's Messenger used to walk on foot to throw pebbles and used to walk back on foot."[86]

## The Prophet Offered the Sacrifice

Jabir, may Allah be pleased with him, narrates: "On the day of the 'Eid of Sacrifice, Allah's Messenger sacrificed two castrated mottled horned rams. When he laid the rams towards the *qibla* for slaughtering, he read the verses,

$$ إِنِّي وَجَّهْتُ وَجْهِيَ لِلَّذِي فَطَرَ السَّمَاوَاتِ $$
$$ وَالْأَرْضَ حَنِيفًا ۖ وَمَا أَنَا مِنَ الْمُشْرِكِينَ $$

*"I have turned my face (my whole being) with pure faith and submission to the One Who has originated the heavens and the earth each with particular features, and I am not one of those associating partners with Allah"*[87] and

---

[85] Muslim, Hajj, 310, 2197; Abu Dawud, Manasik, 78, 1970; Nasai, Hajj, 2220, 5, 270.

[86] Abu Dawud, Manasik, 78, 1969; Tirmidhi, Hajj, 63, 900.

[87] An'am 6:79.

﷽ إِنَّ صَلَاتِي وَنُسُكِي وَمَحْيَايَ وَمَمَاتِي لِلهِ رَبِّ الْعَالَمِينَ

لَا شَرِيكَ لَهُ ۖ وَبِذَلِكَ أُمِرْتُ وَأَنَا أَوَّلُ الْمُسْلِمِينَ

"My Prayer, and all my (other) acts and forms of devotion and worship, and my living and my dying are for Allah alone, the Lord of the worlds. He has no partners; thus have I been commanded, and I am the first and foremost of the Muslims (who have submitted to Him exclusively)."[88] He then slaughtered each ram saying: 'O my Lord! This sacrificial animal is a gift to us from You; we slaughter it for the sake of You, and it (this service) will reach You. O my Lord! Please do accept this from Muhammad and his community. Bismillahi wa'llahu Akbar!'"[89]

## The Prophet Butchered His Animal Himself

Again Jabir, may Allah be pleased with him, narrates: "I was at the presence of the Messenger on a plain assigned for the prayers. When he completed his sermon, he came down from the pulpit. He came and butchered his sacrificial ram himself. While he was conducting this, he said: 'Bismillahi wa'llahu Akbar. This is from me, and in favor of those among my community who cannot offer sacrifice!'"[90]

---

[88] An'am 6:162-163.

[89] Abu Dawud, Dahaya, 4, 2795; Tirmidhi, Adahi, 21, 1520; Ibn Maja, Adahi, 1, 3121.

[90] Tirmidhi, Adahi, 22, 1522.

Ali, may Allah be pleased with him, narrates: "Allah's Messenger slaughtered thirty camels with his own hands. And told me to butcher the rest and I did. They were seventy."[91]

## The Prophet Dispatched Sixty-Three Camels from Medina

Jabir, may Allah be pleased with him, narrates: "Allah's Messenger performed the hajj three times. That is; twice before the hijra, and once after the hijra, at which time he performed it together with umra. (The only obligatory hajj the Messenger performed is after the hijra, and his previous two pilgrimages were before the hajj was enjoined in the Qur'an.) During this hajj (his one and only obligatory hajj, the "Farewell Hajj"), he dispatched from Medina sixty three camels. At that time, Ali, may Allah be pleased with him, came from Yemen with the rest of the sacrificial animals that Allah's Messenger sacrificed. Among these animals was also Abu Jahl's camel, with a silver ring on its nose, which was taken as a gain of war after the Battle of Badr. Allah's Messenger sacrificed them all. Allah's Messenger ordered one piece of meat to be taken from each of the butchered camels. This meat was

---

[91]  Muwatta, Hajj, 181, 1, 394; Abu Dawud, Manasik, 19, 1764.

then cooked in a cauldron, and Allah's Messenger drank from its broth."[92]

## The Prophet Did the Tawaf of Visiting at Night

Ibn Abbas and Aisha, may Allah be pleased with them, narrate: "On the first day of the 'Eid of Sacrifice, Allah's Messenger delayed the *tawaf* of visiting to the night." The *tawaf* that has been ordered with this verse, "*Let them go round the Most Ancient, Honorable House in devotion*,"[93] is the *tawaf* of visiting."[94]

---

[92] Tirmidhi, Hajj, 6, 815.

[93] Hajj 22:29.

[94] Abu Dawud, Manasik, 83, 2000; Tirmidhi, Hajj, 80, 920; Ibn Maja, Manasik, 77, 3059.

## And the Farewell Tawaf

Ibn Abbas, may Allah be pleased with him, narrates: "As the hajj duty finished, the people started to return home. Allah's Messenger said: "Let no one go anywhere until the *Baytu'llah* is the last place he has reached.'"[95] Umar said "The circumambulation of the *Baytu'llah* is the final hajj rite."[96]

---

[95] Muslim, Hajj, 379, 1327; Abu Dawud, Manasik, 84; 2002; Ibn Maja, Manasik, 82, 3070.

[96] Muwatta, Hajj, 1, 369.

# Chapter 4
# How to Practice
# the Hajj and Umra

## Major Pilgrimage

After discussing the wisdom and virtues of the hajj and introducing the Prophet's Farewell Hajj, now we come to the point of giving instructive information about the hajj in detail. To learn instructions about how to perfectly perform the hajj is crucial for those who will carry out this very important pillar of Islam. Without knowing these, one cannot perform the hajj. Even if one were to conduct such a hajj, it could not be considered to be a blessed prayer compliant with the Sunnah of Allah's Messenger. Our beloved Prophet has shown his community how this worship should be fulfilled and said, "Learn your rituals from me." If we want to perform a perfect worship that fully complies with the Sunnah, we have to acquire all this information. If we do not have the opportunity to learn it all, then we must perform our hajj duty under the supervision of an experienced guide.

After these essential warnings, we will now provide practical information that a person who goes on hajj needs.

# A. What Are the Conditions of the Hajj?

Obligatory conditions of the hajj are listed in three main categories:

1- Conditions related to the hajj being obligatory
2- Conditions related to the performance of the hajj
3- Conditions related to the validity of the hajj

## What Conditions Are Required of a Person for the Hajj Duty?

The hajj is obligatory for all free, sane, adult Muslims who have the financial means and are physically capable of performing it. Financial ability includes having sufficient provisions to provide for both themselves and their family for the whole hajj period. Thus, a person intending to go for the hajj should have enough time and financial means to allow him or her to cover all travel expenses and the financial needs of people that they are liable to look after and have left behind.

In addition to these hajj requisites for a person to be regarded as being obliged to perform the hajj, they should have reached the time of fulfilling the hajj prayer. If a person meets all the prequisite conditions of the hajj but dies before the hajj season comes, he or she is counted as having died without having been liable for the hajj.

The hajj duty is conducted during the hajj months, which are *Shawwal, Dhu al-Qa'da* and the first ten days of *Dhu al-Hijja*. Outside of these months, one cannot don the *ihram* for the obligatory hajj duty, nor can one perform the hajj rituals.

Islamic scholars also mention about the security of life, possessions, and travel for the hajj. Scholars of the Hanafi School comment that the verse, *"Pilgrimage to the House is a duty owed to Allah by all who can afford a way to it"* (Imran 3:97), includes the requirement of safe traveling conditions, in addition to the physical and financial capability already mentioned. If one of the conditions that makes the hajj as an obligatory duty is absent, then the hajj duty does not become obligatory to fulfill.

## What Are the Conditions for Performing the Hajj?

The conditions for performing the hajj for a person are as follows:

### a. Having enough strength

A person who is obliged to perform the hajj must have sufficient health to be able to carry out this sacred duty.

Otherwise, a person upon whom the hajj has become an obligation, and who has an illness or a disability that hinders him or her from performing the hajj, should either charge someone to perform the hajj on his or her behalf while he or she is still alive, or request in the will that someone else perform the hajj on his or her behalf after death.

In general, illnesses and disabilities that prevent performing the hajj are listed as follows: blindness, being crippled, paralysis, the absence of feet, a heavy sickness wherein one cannot bear carrying out the rituals of hajj, or extreme old age.

## b. Travel safety

The journey should be secure so that the pilgrims have safe and secure traveling to and from the sacred lands.

## c. Absence of occasions that hinder the hajj

Hajj is not incumbent upon a person so long as there is a casual reason that prevents a person from going on the hajj during the season of hajj, such as imprisonment or being subject to a prohibition against going abroad. As for the conditions peculiar to female pilgrims, which ban women from setting off on any long journey unaccompanied by a *mahram*, an unmarriageable male, there is an added condition of going on the hajj together with her husband or a close male relative who has reached adulthood, such as her father, son, brother, uncle, nephew. According to the general view, for unaccompanied women to go on the hajj from a distance more than 90 km is not seen as permissible. In some different evaluations (according to the Shafii School, for instance), it is not the distance but mainly travel security and the woman's safety which must be taken as the fundamental requirement. Thus, according to this view, the presence of the husband or any close male relative is not accepted as a principal condition for women to go on the hajj, so that a group of at least three women—or even one women on her own, if she feels secure enough—is allowed to go for the hajj without a *mahram*. In any case it is important to follow up the regulations to get a travel visa to Mecca.

In summary, those who are liable to go for the hajj must perform the hajj themselves or must send a representative on their behalf, or must request this in their will.

## What Are the Conditions in Order for the Hajj to Be Valid?

The three obligations of the hajj are as follows:

1- Entering into the state of *ihram* with the intention of performing the hajj
2- Performing the hajj at a particular time of the year
3- Being at specified place

## What Does *Ihram* Mean?

In dictionaries, as the word "*ihram*" means depriving and forbidding oneself of certain things, it also means reaching a time or place which should be respected and paying respect to these values. Thus, for those who make intention of performing the hajj or umra until all the rites of hajj or umra are completed, the term "*ihram*" means depriving themselves of some actions and deeds which are normally allowed at other times.

Some deeds which are allowed at other times become forbidden for those who entered into the state of *ihram*. Violations of these prohibitions—as related to garments, outward appearance, sexual life, and hunting—require penalties in accordance with the type of prohibition and the way in which the violation took place. Penalties include sacrificing an animal, giving alms, and fasting a certain number of days. *Ihram* is also publicly known as the garment that is composed of two pieces of cotton cloth without any stitches. *Ihram* happens when one covers himself with this cloth together with the intention for the hajj or umra and *talbiya*.

## What Are the Essentials of *Ihram*?

According to the Hanafi School, *ihram* has two essentials: intention and *talbiya*. Absence of only one of these conditions invalidates entering into *ihram*.

Intention means to decide to perform the whole hajj or umra. Intention is mainly conducted by the heart. With the condition of being heartfully aware, during which words of intention are said, expressing the intention with the tongue is also regarded as a good deed. If the pilgrims are doing *hajj tamattu* (combining the hajj and umra with a break in between), they can make their statement of intention, as follows: "O Allah! Only for Your pleasure and Your sake, I intend to perform umra! Please ease this worship for me, and accept it from me."

When the intention is stated and the *talbiya* is recited, a person is then regarded as having formally entered into the state of *ihram*. The *talbiya* itself is a recitation of this prayer: "*Labbayk Allahumma labbayk, Labbayk la sharika laka labbayk, Inna'l-hamda wa'n-ni'mata laka wa'l-mulk, La sharika lak.*" This *talbiya* can be translated as follows: "Here I am, O Allah, at Your command! Here I am at Your command! You are without associate! Here I am at Your command! Yours are praise, grace and dominion! You are without associate!"

To recite the *talbiya* once while entering into *ihram* is an obligation, and to repeat it loudly every so often is *sunnah*. It is worth noting that women should not raise their voices loudly while reciting the *talbiya*, nor while saying prayers, remembering or glorifying Allah.

## When should one enter into ihram?

Hajj rites cannot be performed before the months of hajj. According to the Hanafi School, entering into *ihram* before the hajj months begin is allowable, but it is *makruh* (detested) because *ihram* is not one of the pillars of hajj but rather a condition for its validity and correctness. As with other acts of worship, it is not necessary for the time of prayer to come to render the condition.

According to the Shafii School, however, *ihram* is regarded as a pillar of hajj, not merely as a condition; thus, according to this view, it is not allowed to enter into *ihram* before the months of hajj. If one gets into the state of *ihram* before the hajj months, this *ihram* will be regarded as *ihram* for umra only. Since there is not an appointed time for umra, people can enter into *ihram* for umra anytime they like.

## Where are the places where one can enter into ihram?

A *miqat* is a specific geographic location for entering into *ihram*. As a term, *miqat* points to certain special places around Mecca where pilgrims coming from different directions must enter into a state of *ihram*. In the Holy Qur'an, the Ka'ba is described as the *Bayt al-Haram* (the Sacred House);[97] the mosque around the Ka'ba is named the

---

[97] Maedah 5:2

*Masjid al-Haram* (the Sacred Mosque);[98] the city surrounding the Ka'ba and its environ is called simply the *Haram* (a secure sanctuary),[99] thus the Ka'ba and the surrounding area are identified as worthy of high respect and a place of dignity. The area surrounding the Ka'ba is divided into three regions which are known as the *Haram*; the *Hill*, and the *Afaq*, with respect to their closeness to the Ka'ba. Thus, the various positions of people who will make intention for the hajj and umra vary according to their specific location with respect to these regions.

## The Haram Region

The *Haram* is the region of security and safety that covers the Ka'ba and the surroundings, where cutting plants, disturbing the natural environment, harming animals, and interfering with the lives of its living beings is prohibited. Its borders were defined by Prophet Abraham, peace be upon him, under the instructions of Gabriel, and later redefined by our noble Prophet.

Dwellers of Mecca can enter into *ihram* for the hajj within the borders of the *Haram*, but they have to go out of these borders to enter into the state of *ihram* for umra by going to Arafat or Tan'im, the closest places to the *Hill* region.

---

[98] Isra 17:1

[99] Qasas 28:57; Ankabut 29:67.

## The Hill Region

This is the region between the *Haram* and the places of *miqat*. People living in this region enter into *ihram* from where they are, outside the borders of the *Haram*.

## The Afaq Region

All places apart from those covered by the regions of the *Haram* and the *Hill* are called the *Afaq*. The five places from where pilgrims who come to Mecca or the *Haram* region from the *Afaq* cannot pass without entering into *ihram* were defined by Allah's Messenger. Dwellers of *Afaq* region are called "*Afaqi*."

These five points, where people who come to Mecca al-Mukarrama or the *Haram* region cannot pass without getting into the state of *ihram*, are as follows:

*Dhu al-Hulayfa*: It is the *miqat* for those who come from the direction of Medina. It is at a distance of 10 km from Medina and 450 km to Mecca. This is the farthest *miqat* from Mecca. Our Blessed Prophet entered into *ihram* in this *miqat* when he intended to perform his farewell hajj.

*Juhfa (Rabigh)*: This is the *miqat* for those who come from the direction of Egypt and Syria. It is at a distance of 187 km to Mecca.

*Dhat Iraq*: This is the *miqat* for those coming from the direction of Iraq, and it is 94 km away from Mecca.

*Yalamlam:* This is the *miqat* for those coming from the direction of Yemen and India. Being only 54 km away from Mecca, it is the closest *miqat* to Mecca.

*Qarn al-Manazil:* This is the *miqat* of those coming from the direction of Najd and Kuwait. It is at a distance of 96 km from Mecca.

Those who fly to Jiddah should enter *ihram* on the plane before they pass over the *miqat* which is applicable to the direction they are coming from. However, because it will be difficult for them to enter *ihram* on the plane, as a more correct practice, pilgrims should enter into *ihram* in the airport.

## Is it allowed to enter the Haram region without being in a state of ihram?

The *Afaqis* who come directly to the *Haram* region from far distances for any reason should enter into *ihram* before they pass the respective *miqat* border. *Afaqis* are those who come to Mecca from outside all *miqat* borders. Entering into *ihram* has been made an obligation for exhibiting respect to this sacred region. In this regard, there is no difference between those who come here for the hajj or umra, and those who come for other purposes, such as visiting or trading. Those who come to the *Haram* region for pilgrimage come out of *ihram* after performing the hajj prayer or umra visit. Dwellers of the *Hill* and *Haram* regions who are outside the borders of *miqat* for any reason are also subject to the same rules which apply to the *afaqis*.

According to the Shafii School, for *afaqis* (i.e., those who come from long distances) without having any intention of performing the hajj or umra to enter the *Haram* region with *ihram* is not necessary, but rather, something strongly recommended.

When they will not perform the hajj or umra, dwellers of the *Hill* region can go in and out of the *Haram* region without *ihram*. When they go to the *Hill* region—for example, to Jiddah—Meccans and the *afaqis* who are present in the *Haram* region can return to the *Haram* region without *ihram*. In the absence of the intention of going directly to the *Haram* region, *afaqis* who will go to any other place—Jiddah, for example—are not required to pass the *miqat* border in a state of *ihram*. But if such people want to go to the *Haram* region—to Mecca, for example—then they become subject to the rules which apply to those who dwell in the Hill region. If they do not intend to perform the hajj or umra, they can enter the *Haram* region without *ihram* and make *tawaf* around the Ka'ba without donning *ihram* clothes.

After pilgrims land in Jiddah, if those who pass the *miqat* border without *ihram* in order to visit Medina before performing the hajj will have to go to Mecca first, they enter *ihram* before they can cross the border of the *Haram* region into Mecca.

## What are the necessities (wajib acts) of ihram?

a. *Not to cross the borders of miqat without ihram:* If the *afaqis* (those who live outside the borders of the *miqat*) cross the *miqat* without *ihram*, they have to pay an expiation which consists of sacrificing a sheep or a goat. However, if those *afaqis* who pass the *miqat* border without *ihram* go back to the *miqat* border and enter into *ihram* there before starting any of the rites of the hajj or umra (before starting to perform the "*tawaf* of arrival" or "*umra tawaf*," for example), then they do not have to pay this penalty. Such people can also go to a *miqat* border that is closer to where they are and enter into *ihram* there. However, if one of the rites of hajj or umra started after a person crossed the *miqat* border without *ihram*, even if she or he returns to the *miqat* border, she or he will still have to pay this penalty.

b. *Abstaining from the prohibitions which apply to the state of ihram:* This means staying away from every deed and action that does not comply with the high spirit and sublime meaning of the hajj. These disapproved actions will be explained in the section on *ihram* prohibitions.

## What are the sunnah acts of being in ihram?

Before entering into *ihram*, that is before making the intention and reciting the *talbiya*, the following are *sunnah* acts:

- to attain a state of general cleanliness by cutting nails, shaving armpit and pubic hair, and for males, trimming the hair, if necessary
- taking a whole-body, or prayer, ablution
- wearing pleasant perfumes (without alcohol)
- to be wrapped with seamless cloak called an *izar* and *rida*, that is made of two pieces of white thin towel, one of which covers the lower body while the other covers the top part (this is obviously for males only as females can wear normal clothing, provided that it is clean and relatively loose-fitting, and that it covers all the parts of body as required.)
- After getting into the state of *ihram*, if it is not *karaha*, times when the performance of prayers is banned, the pilgrim should perform two rak'ats of *ihram* prayer. After *Sura Fatiha* in the first rak'at, the pilgrim should read *Sura Kafirun*; and after reading *Sura Fatiha* in the second rak'at, the pilgrim should read *Sura Ikhlas*. They should also recite the *talbiya* at any possible time.

### What are the prohibitions which apply to the state of ihram?

Prohibitions of the state of *ihram* can be grouped as follows:

Prohibitions related to the body of the person who entered into *ihram*:

- To have one's hair cut, and for males, shortening the beard or moustache
- Shaving, plucking, or breaking off any hair on the body, or cutting nails
- For the purpose of looking attractive, dying, oiling, wearing gel on the hair, wearing perfume, using perfumed soap, or, for women, putting on make up, etc.

Prohibitions related to garments and clothes:

- Prohibited for men only are clothing that are sewn or knitted for the purpose of dressing up; covering the head (prohibited for men only) and face (prohibited for men and women); wearing a *takka* (cap) or other similar headdress; turbans; gloves; socks; or shoes that cover the heels. However, wearing over-the-shoulders type of outerwear, like coats is permissible. Also, belts worn on the waist, bags, slippers or shoes that do not cover the heels and toes can have stitches.

- Females can wear normal clothing, provided that it is clean and relatively loose-fitting, and that it covers the arms to the wrist and the legs to the ankle; and while they must cover their heads, they do not cover their faces during the period of *ihram*.

Prohibitions related to sexual matters:

- Sexual relations and actions like kissing, toying or holding with desire—in short, any and all

actions that generally lead to sexual intercourse—
are completely prohibited.

- Speaking words that invoke lusty feelings is also
forbidden.

Prohibitions related to the *Haram* region:

- Hunting game animals; and cutting, picking or
plucking plants and flowers in and around Mecca
al-Mukarrama (the region of the *Haram*) are actions
which are forbidden for everyone, whether or
not they are in a state of *ihram*.

Prohibitions related to the rights of others and sinful actions:

- *Fusuq*: Receding from obeying commands and
prohibitions defined by Allah and committing
actions that are regarded as sinful

- *Jidal*: Quarrelling, fighting, insulting, breaking
hearts with harsh and bad words and deeds, causing disturbances (Especially while in *ihram*, people must stay away from any behaviors that may
raise disquiet and harm the general social tranquility.)

- Killing or hunting any animal, whether its meat
is edible or not, including showing an animal to
a hunter, helping a hunter, or causing any harm
to any animal

## *What are the actions that are not prohibited for those in a state of ihram?*

- To be shaded or to use umbrella
- To change the *ihram* clothes into another set of ihram clothes
- To wash oneself or use odorless soap
- To brush teeth or to wear kohl
- To have a tooth taken out, to give blood, to receive an injection, or to put a bandage over an injury
- To pull out a broken nail or a harming hair
- To carry a weapon, or to wear a bracelet, ring or watch
- To wear a belt or carry a bag on one's shoulder
- To smell a flower or a fruit
- To be in a shop selling scents and perfumes or to buy a scent
- To be covered with a blanket or a duvet without covering the head (males only) or face (males and females)
- To put a coat over the shoulders only, without putting one's arms in the sleeves

## Specified Time

This is the condition required for the validity of the hajj related to performing the rituals of hajj, like entering into ihram, standing at Arafat, and conducting the "*tawaf* of visiting," all at their particular appointed times. The hajj rites are performed during the months of Shawwal, Dhu al-Qa'da, and in the first ten days of Dhu al-Hijja. Before reaching these months, the hajj rites cannot be performed. Each hajj rite (the standing at Arafat, circumambulating the Ka'ba, striding between Safa and Marwa, and stoning Satan) must be performed at times that are defined within these months; otherwise the hajj worship cannot be considered valid.

## Specified Places

The obligations of hajj must be fulfilled at particular places. That is, the standing must be conducted within the boundaries of Arafat, and the circumambulation must be performed around the Ka'ba, within the boundaries of the Masjid al-Haram.

# B. What Are the Essentials of Hajj?

According to the Hanafi School, the hajj has three principal obligations; these are entering into the state of *ihram*; the standing at Arafat; and the "*tawaf* of visiting." Of these obligations, going into the state of consecration, known as *ihram*, is the prerequisite (*shart*); while the standing at Arafat and the "*tawaf* of visiting" are the hajj essentials (*rukns*). Since standing at Arafat, as one of the essentials (*rukns*), is limited to a specified time, a person who misses the time of standing at Arafat will be deprived of performing the hajj that year. In this case, he or she will have to go for the hajj again another year.

It is an obligation to perform the first three essentials (*rukns*) in sequence. According to the Shafii School, however, in addition to these three obligations, striding between Safa and Marwa, and shaving off or shortening the hair are also considered among the essentials (*rukns*) of the hajj.

If all of the hajj essentials are not fulfilled in full compliance to their procedures and conditions, the hajj is not valid, even if the person pays expiation (*kaffara*). The conditions that render the validity of the hajj prayer were discussed earlier. Now, we will explain the hajj essentials of standing at Arafat and the "*tawaf* of visiting."

## Standing at Arafat

Standing at Arafat, an essential without which the hajj cannot be valid, is performed within the defined region of Arafat that is outside the *Haram* region and is situated about 25 km southeast of Mecca.

What this rite actually means is being present on the plains of Arafat for some time. The hadith, "Hajj is Arafat,"[100] indicates the importance of the standing at

---

[100] Tirmidhi, Tafsir, 3; Abu Dawud, Manasik, 68; Ibn Maja, Manasik, 57.

Arafat and warns us to be very careful not to miss this essential of the hajj prayer. In this regard, those who cannot carry out the duty of standing at Arafat during the hajj will have to set out anew to fulfill this prayer in the following hajj seasons.

## Which conditions are required in order for the Standing at Arafat to be valid?

– To be in the state of *ihram* with the intention of performing the hajj

– To perform the standing within the defined boundaries of the Arafat plain on the Day of Arafat (the eve of the Eid), within the period of time from the time of noon on the eve of the Eid until the dawn of the Eid day (i.e. the time of the Morning Prayer of the next day).

The UranaValley is the border of Arafat in the direction of Mecca. Apart from the UranaValley, the standing can be fulfilled anywhere in the Arafat region. This valley is not counted as part of the Arafat region. Some parts of the northwest section of the Namira Mosque, which is situated in this valley, also remain outside the standing place. To fulfill the standing on the lower slopes of the hill called *Jabal ar-Rahma* is a *sunnah* practice. The time for the standing at Arafat begins as the sun reaches the peak height on the Day of Arafat (the Eve of the Eid)—that is, the ninth day of the month of Dhu al-Hijja—and it ends as the dawn of the Eid day breaks. Neither making the intention nor being aware of being present at Arafat is a condition for the validity of this standing worship. All pilgrims, whether they are conscious or unconscious, sleeping or awake, or have ablution or not—in other words, in any condition—who have been within the Arafat boundaries, even for a very short while, are regarded as having performed the standing at Arafat. However, those who reach Arafat in the daytime on the Day of Arafat are strongly recommended not to leave Arafat before sunset. If a pilgrim leaves Arafat without any justifiable excuse, but comes back before sunset, he does not need to do anything in recompense; otherwise, he has to sacrifice a sheep or a goat. According to the Shafii School, no expiation is applied to those who leave Arafat before sunset.

*What are the sunnah acts of the Standing at Arafat?*

- To spend the night that connects the Day of *Tarwiya* (the eighth day of Dhu al-Hijja) to the Day of Arafat in Mina, and then proceed to Arafat on the Day of Arafat after the sunrise

- To be on Arafat before the sunset and, if possible, after having a bath

- Attending the sermon in the Namira Mosque given right after the sinking of the sun after noon and before performing the Noon Prayer

- To perform the Noon and Afternoon Prayers together at the noon time
- While standing at Arafat, to be in a state of ablution and to face towards the Ka'ba
- To perform the standing (*wuquf*) after the noon and afternoon prayers are performed together
- Not to be fasting on the Day of Arafat
- To spend most of the day reciting the *talbiya* and reading the *tasbih*; and to engage in *dhikr*, supplication, sincere imploring and repentance (*istighfar*)
- To perform the standing (*wuquf*) at a place as close as possible to *Jabal ar-Rahma*, the Hill of Mercy

While fulfilling the duty of being present at Arafat, standing up is more virtuous than sitting down, and being mounted on an animal is more virtuous than standing up.

The term, *jam at-taqdim*, means to perform the noon and afternoon prayers one after the other, at the time for the noon prayer while standing at Arafat on the Day of Arafat. This is a *sunnah* practice. When the call for prayer is recited at the noon time, first the initial *sunnah* of the noon prayer is performed. Then, after the *iqama*, the *fard* of the noonprayer is performed in congregation. After this, another *iqama* is read and the *fard* of the afternoon prayer is performed. Another call (*adhan*) for afternoon prayer is not recited and *sunnah* prayers between the two prescribed (*fard*) prayers are not performed. After each prescribed (*fard*) prayer, *talbiyas* are recited and *tashriq takbirs* are read aloud.

## The "Tawaf of Visiting"

The second essential of the hajj is the "*tawaf* of visiting." Without performing the "*tawaf* of visiting," the hajj cannot be completed. The obligation of performing the "*tawaf* of visiting" is commanded in the Qur'an with this verse,

ثُمَّ لْيَقْضُوا تَفَثَهُمْ وَلْيُوفُوا نُذُورَهُمْ وَلْيَطَّوَّفُوا بِالْبَيْتِ الْعَتِيقِ

*"Then let them tidy themselves up (by having their hair cut, removing their ihram (Hajj attire), taking a bath, and clipping their nails, etc.) and fulfill their vows (if they have made any, and complete other acts of the Pilgrimage) and go round the Most Ancient, Honorable House in devotion"* (al-Hajj 22:27).

*Tawaf* means to circumambulate or to go around something. As one of the hajj rites, *tawaf* designates the act of circumambulating the Ka'ba seven times, beginning from the Ka'ba's corner, or the direction where the *Hajar al-Aswad* is situated. Each turn is called one round (*shawt*), and a set of seven rounds (*shawts*) makes one *tawaf*.

### Which conditions are required in order for the circumambulation to be valid?

For a *tawaf* to be complete or valid, it must be performed within the specified time for the *tawaf*. The "*tawaf* of visiting" is also called *tawaf al-ifada*. The time of the "*tawaf* of visiting" begins at the dawn of the first day of Eid. Although the "*tawaf* of visiting" can be performed any time between the dawn of the first day of the Eid of Sacrifice until the end of one's life, according to Abu Hanifa, it must be fulfilled prior to sunset on the third day of the Eid.

According to the Shafii School, the time of the "*tawaf* of visiting" begins at midnight on the Day of Arafat, and although it is *sunnah* to fulfill this *tawaf* within the first three days of the Eid, to perform the "*tawaf* of visiting" on the first day of the Eid is more virtuous.

Although it is enough to declare the intention in one's heart, it is recommended that pilgrims make the intention both verbally and in their hearts. Walking around the Ka'ba without intending to make *tawaf* is not regarded as *tawaf*.

While making the intention for *tawaf*, it is not necessary to declare whether this intention is for the "*tawaf* of arrival," in Mecca; the "*tawaf* of visiting," after coming from Mina; or the *tawaf*, for *umra*. To simply make the intention for performing *tawaf* is adequate. It is essential for *tawaf* to be performed within the *Masjid al-Haram*, around the Ka'ba. People can also make *tawaf* from the upper levels of the *Masjid al-Haram*. The *tawaf* cannot be made from outside the *Masjid al-Haram*.

To complete more than half of the rounds (*shawts*) is also one of the conditions of validity for the *tawaf*. According to the Hanafi School, to complete at least four rounds is necessary for a *tawaf* to be valid. As for the obligatory (*fard*) or necessary (*wajib*) *tawafs*, an expiation applies for every missing round (*shawt*).

## What are the necessities (wajib acts) of circumambulation?

- To have ablution and to keep this ablution while performing *tawaf* (If the ablution is ruined during the *tawaf*, after renewing it, one can complete the missing rounds of *tawaf*.)
- Parts of body that are regarded private must be covered. If one fourth or more of these private parts is uncovered during *tawaf*, an expiation is applied.
- To start the *tawaf* from the line of the *Hajar al-Aswad*
- To perform the *tawaf* by keeping the Ka'ba on the left side
- To circumambulate the Ka'ba by walking outside the *Hatim*, the wall of the *Hijr* (This is necessary for the *tawaf*, as the *Hijr*, the semi-circular compound towards the north of the Ka'ba, is counted as being a part of the Ka'ba.)
- To complete *fard* and *wajib tawafs* with the set of seven circuits

- For those who are able, to circumambulate the Ka'ba by walking by himself or herself
- To perform the *tawaf* prayer after completing a *tawaf* (Whether it is an obligatory or supererogatory *tawaf*, to perform two *rak'ats* of *tawaf* prayer at the end of every sets of seven circuits is an obligation.)

## What are the sunnah acts of circumambulation?

- To be purified from all impurities, both on the body and on the *ihram* clothes, that may prevent one from performing the prayers
- While starting the *tawaf*, to come to the *Hajar al-Aswad* or to its direction from the side of the Yemeni corner
- To salute the *Hajar al-Aswad* at the beginning of the *tawaf* and at the end of every *shawt*. When starting the *tawaf*, and each time they pass in front of the *Hajar al-Aswad*, pilgrims pause and hold their hands up next to ears, say a *takbir* of *Allahu Akbar* ("Allah is the Greatest!") and recite the *tahlil*. The *tahlil* is a recitation of these words: "*La ilaha illa'llahu wahdahu la sharika lah, lahul mulku wa lahul hamd, wa huwa ala kulli shayin qadir*" ("There is no deity but Allah, One with no partner. His is the absolute property and dominion (of the universe), and to Him is due and

belong all praise and gratitude; and He is All-Powerful over everything.") If it is possible, the *Hajar al-Aswad* can be kissed or touched. However, in cases when it is not possible to get near the *Hajar al-Aswad* due to crowding, and in order to avoid disturbing other people, one can salute the *Hajar al-Aswad* from a distance with the palms facing towards the Ka'ba, by holding up the hands next to the ears and saying, "*Bismillahi Allahu Akbar.*" After saluting like this, the pilgrim can kiss the palm of his or her right hand. Further, while saluting the *Hajar al-Aswad* from a long distance, a pilgrim does not have to pause but can just carry on walking.

It is very important not to cause any hardship for people while trying to salute the *Hajar al-Aswad* because our Blessed Prophet, mounted on his camel, saluted the *Hajar al-Aswad* with the stick he was holding and then kissed the stick.[101] Moreover, Allah's Messenger warned his Companions about this matter. He told Umar, "O Umar! You have much power. While saluting the *Hajar al-Aswad*, do not ever cause trouble for the weak ones by squashing them. If you have the opportunity to walk close to it and stroke it, do it; but if you do not have such an opportunity, then salute it from a distance and recite

---

[101] Muslim, Hajj, 257.

the *takbir* and *tahlil* when you come opposite the *Hajar al-Aswad*."[102] It is recommended (*mustahab*) to salute the *Hajar al-Aswad* from the *Rukn al-Yemeni* (the corner of the Ka'ba which contains the *Hajar al-Aswad*).

- To make *raml* in the first three rounds of the circumambulation(*Raml* is a way of walking briskly accompanied by movements of the arms and legs to show one's physical strength. *Raml* is performed by the men only and not by the women.)

- To make *idhtiba* for men during *tawafs* in which making *raml* is necessary—*Idhtiba* means to place the end of the *ihram* covering the top part of the body over the left shoulder, and to leave the right shoulder uncovered. In all *tawafs* in which the *raml* is made, to make *idhtiba* is *sunnah*. When the first three rounds are finished, the shoulder is covered and the prayer of *tawaf* is performed while both shoulders are covered. To make *idhtiba* in times other than *tawafs* with *raml* is reprehensible (*makruh*).

- To perform all seven rounds of a *tawaf* one after the other is *sunnah*. In case the completing of the *tawaf* is prevented—such as by the *adhan* for a *fard* prayer to be read, or when ablution is broken while performing the *tawaf*—the *tawaf* is

---

[102] Ahmad ibn Hanbal, Musnad, 1/28; Bayhaqi, Sunan al-Kubra, 5/80.

terminated and the rest of the rounds are completed later.

- It is *sunnah* for men to make the *tawaf* from closer rings of the Ka'ba and for women to walk around the outer rings as much as possible.

- It is reprehensible (*makruh*) not to perform the *sunnah* acts of *tawaf* without any justifiable excuse. Although they lose a great amount of reward, those who do not perform *sunnah* acts are not subject to any expiation, however.

## How is the Ka'ba circumambulated?

A person who would like to perform a *tawaf* lines up with the *Hajar al-Aswad* from the side of the *Rukn al-Yemeni* and makes the proper intention. After saluting the *Hajar al-Aswad* by saying, "Bismillahi Allahu Akbar," the pilgrim starts to circumambulate the Ka'ba.

During the circumambulation, pilgrims read *takbirs* and *tahlils* as well as *salawat* to Allah's Messenger. At each round, they salute the *Hajar al-Aswad*. After circumambulating the Ka'ba seven times, two *rak'ats* of *tawaf* prayer is performed, if possible, behind the Station of Abraham—if not, then at any suitable place. (Our Prophet performed two *rak'ats* of prayer at the Station of Abraham and read *Sura Kafirun* and *Sura Ikhlas* during this prayer.) They complete the *tawaf* after their supplication following the prayer.

## What are the different types of circumambulations of the Ka'ba?

Apart from the "*tawaf* of visiting," which is an essential of the hajj, there are obligatory (*fard*), necessary (*wajib*), and *sunnah tawafs*. However, all *tawafs* are performed in the same manner. Some *tawafs* are related to, while others are not.

*Tawafs* that are related to the hajj are the "*tawaf* of arrival," in Mecca; the "*tawaf* of visiting"; and the "farewell *tawaf*." The *tawaf* that is performed during umra is called the "*tawaf* of umra."

Following are descriptions of the types of circumambulations of the Ka'ba that are not related to the hajj or umra.

1- *The circumambulation of the Ka'ba to fulfill a vow*: If a person made a vow to perform *tawaf*, it is an obligation for this person to fulfill his vow. If he defined a certain time for his *tawaf*, then he must perform this *tawaf* at the specified time. If there is not any defined time, then he should perform his circumambulation of the Ka'ba to fulfill the vow at any suitable time.

2- *The "Circumambulation of Greeting" (Tawaf of tahiyyat al-masjid)*: It is *sunnah* to perform two *rak'ats* of *tahiyyat al-masjid* (greeting) prayer when one enters a mosque. When one enters the *Masjid al-Haram*, however, it is strongly recommended to make a *tawaf* to greet the most sublime *masjid* on Earth. This *tawaf* is called the "*tawaf* of *tahiyyat al-masjid*," which means the "*tawaf* of greeting." The *tawaf* that is performed for the hajj and umra is also regarded as the "*tawaf* of greeting."

3- *Supererogatory circumambulations of the Ka'ba:* While in Mecca, apart from the circumambulations of the Ka'ba to fulfill the rites of hajj or umra, other circumambulations of the Ka'ba that are performed at any opportunity are called supererogatory circumambulations.

## C. What Are the Necessities of the Hajj?

Apart from the essentials and conditions of the hajj, there are the hajj rites which are necessary (*wajib*). Not performing these will not invalidate the hajj prayer. However, not performing these necessary (*wajib*) duties without any justifiable excuse is strongly detested (*tahriman makruh*). Worshippers who do not perform the necessities (*wajib* acts) without any justifiable excuse, or miss the time for performing *wajib* acts are subject to expiation.

The necessities of the hajj are listed in two groups as primary and secondary *wajib* acts:

1- *Primary wajib acts:* These are composed of the five hajj rites: striding between the hills of Safa and Marwa; the standing at Muzdalifa; stoning Satan (*ram al-jimar*); shaving off or shortening the hair; and performing the "farewell *tawaf*."

2- *Secondary wajib acts:* These can be listed as the *wajib* acts of *ihram*; the *wajib* acts of *tawaf*; the *wajib* acts of the striding between the hills of Safa and Marwa; the *wajib* acts of the standing at Arafat; the *wajib* acts of Muzdalifa; and the *wajib* acts of Mina. All these secondary *wajib* duties will be detailed below under the related title.

## Striding Between Safa and Marwa

*Sa'y* literally means "running, spending effort." As a term, *sa'y* means to stride seven times between the hills of Safa and Marwa, starting from Safa and ending in Marwa, four times there and three times back. Each striding from Safa to Marwa is considered to be a lap, and each striding from Marwa to Safa is considered to be a second lap. This span of about 350 meters where the *sa'y* is fulfilled is called the *mas'a* (the running place).

In the Qur'an, the importance of *sa'y* is emphasized in the following verse:

$$\text{إِنَّ الصَّفَا وَالْمَرْوَةَ مِن شَعَائِرِ اللهِ ۖ فَمَنْ حَجَّ الْبَيْتَ أَوِ اعْتَمَرَ فَلَا جُنَاحَ عَلَيْهِ أَن يَطَّوَّفَ بِهِمَا ۚ وَمَن تَطَوَّعَ خَيْرًا فَإِنَّ اللهَ شَاكِرٌ عَلِيمٌ}$$

(The hills of) Safa and Marwa are among the emblems Allah has appointed (to represent Islam and the Muslim community). Hence, whoever does the Hajj to the House (of Allah, the Ka'ba) or the Umra, there is no blame on him to run between them (and let them run after they go round the Ka'ba as an obligatory rite). And whoever does a good deed voluntarily (such as an additional going-round the Ka'ba or running between Safa and Marwa, and other kinds of good deeds), surely Allah is All-Responsive to thankfulness, All-Knowing. (Al-Baqarah 2:158).

## What are the conditions of validity for the sa'y?

The conditions that render a *sa'y* valid are briefly listed as follows:

- To perform sa'y after entering into *ihram*, that is, after making the intention for the hajj or umra and reciting the *talbiya*. None of the hajj rites can be performed before one enters into the state of *ihram*. For a *sa'y* to be regarded as valid and correct—and although it is essential to perform the *sa'y* after entering into the state of *ihram*— it is not compulsory to perform the *sa'y* with *ihram* clothes. The *sa'y* can be performed after completing some rites and the pilgrim comes out of *ihram*. As a person who enters into *ihram* for the hajj cannot come out of *ihram* before the dawn of the first day of the Eid of Sacrifice, if he wants to perform the *sa'y* before the standing at Arafat, then he has to perform the *sa'y* while wearing the *ihram* clothes. However, if one performs the *sa'y* after returning from Arafat and after the "*tawaf* of visiting*," then he can perform the *sa'y* while out of the *ihram* clothes—this is the most virtuous way of performing *sa'y* and it complies best with *sunnah*. To perform *umra sa'y* with *ihram* is necessary (*wajib*). A person who shaves after the fourth lap of the *umra sa'y* is regarded as having come out of *ihram*. The *sa'y* that is performed by this person without *ihram* is valid, but since he abandoned performing a *wajib* act, an expiation applies to him.

– To perform the hajj *sa'y* after the hajj months begin. Apart from entering *ihram*, none of the hajj rites can be performed before the hajj months begin.

– To perform the *sa'y* after an accepted (*mu'tabar*) *tawaf*. The *sa'y* is not a hajj ritual on its own. *Mu'tabar tawaf*, on the other hand, means a *tawaf* that is not performed in a situation that cancels the validity of *tawaf*, such as the occasions that necessitate having a bath, or for women, during menstruation or postpartum bleeding.

– To have completed most (at least four) of the laps. According to the Hanafi School, four laps of seven *sa'y* are essential (*rukn*) and three are necessary (*wajib*). According to the other three schools, however, all laps are essential, which means that all laps have to be completed.

- To start the *sa'y* from Safa. If the *sa'y* is started from Marwa, it is not regarded as correct or valid.

## What are the necessities (wajib acts) of the sa'y?

- To perform the *sa'y* on foot (Those who cannot perform the *sa'y* by walking due to reasons like old age, weakness or disability, can perform it with a carriage.)
- To complete the *sa'y* with seven laps

## What are the sunnah acts of the sa'y?

- To perform the *sa'y* straight after the circumambulation of the Ka'ba
- To perform the *sa'y* with ablution
- Not to have any impurities, either on the body or on the clothes, that prevents one from performing the prayers
- To salute the *Hajar al-Aswad* before starting the *sa'y*
- At the end of each lap, to climb so high up the hills that the Ka'ba can be seen
- To perform the laps one after the other, without any break

- For men, to walk fast and boldly (*harwala*) between pillars that are indicated with green lights
- To be engaged in reading *takbirs*, *tahlils* and saying prayers and invocations during the performance of the *sa'y*

## How is the sa'y performed?

After the circumambulation is performed, pilgrims go to Safa. *Hajar al-Aswad* is saluted and intention is made for the *sa'y* either for the hajj or umra with these words: "O my Allah! Only for Your acceptance, do I seek to perform the hajj (or umra) *sa'y* composed of seven laps between Safa and Marwa. Please ease this task for me and accept it from me." Reciting *takbirs*, *tahlils*, the remembrance of Allah, and supplications, pilgrims walk towards Marwa. During the fast walking between green-lighted pillars, this supplication is said: "O my Lord! Please forgive my sins; bestow Your Compassion over us; please overlook and cover our faults; honor and grant us from Your Endless Generosity; forgive and clear all our sins, for You know all what we do not know. Verily You are the most Sublime, the most Generous." When four laps from Safa to Marwa, and three return laps from Marwa to Safa are completed, it means that one *sa'y* has been completed.

The *sa'y* is not an independent prayer on its own. It must definitely be performed after a *tawaf*. The *sa'y* is performed separately for the hajj and umra. There is no supererogatory *sa'y*. Hence, the *sa'y* is not performed after each circumambulation of the Ka'ba.

## The Standing at Muzdalifa

The standing at Muzdalifa is fulfilled within the boundaries of Muzdalifa. Muzdalifa is the name of a region that remains between Mina and Arafat, within the boundaries of the *Haram* region. During the hajj, to spend the night that connects the Day of Arafat to the Eid Day in this region is a *sunnah* act and to perform the standing here after the morning prayer is necessary (*wajib*).

### What are the conditions of validity for the Standing at Muzdalifa?

- To go into the state of *ihram* with the intention of fulfilling the hajj duty
- To have completed the standing at Arafat
- To perform the standing within the specified boundaries of Muzdalifa (To be present for the standing around *Mash'ar al-Haram* is *sunnah*.)
- To perform the standing within the specified period of time

### When is the Standing at Muzdalifa performed?

The standing at Muzdalifa can be fulfilled on the first day of the Eid from the first dawn, the onset of the time of the Morning Prayer, until the sunrise.

As it is the case for the standing at Arafat, pilgrims who have been on Muzdalifa within this specified time, even for only a short moment, conscious or unconscious, sleeping or awake, are regarded as having fulfilled the standing at Muzdalifa.

In the Qur'an, the standing at Muzdalifa is emphasized in the following verse:

فَإِذَا أَفَضْتُم مِّنْ عَرَفَاتٍ فَاذْكُرُوا اللَّهَ عِندَ الْمَشْعَرِ الْحَرَامِ ۖ وَاذْكُرُوهُ كَمَا هَدَاكُمْ وَإِن كُنتُم مِّن قَبْلِهِ لَمِنَ الضَّالِّينَ

When you press on in multitude from Arafat (after you have stayed there for some time), mention Allah at Mash'ar al-Haram (al-Muzdalifa); mention Him aware of how He has guided you, for formerly you were surely of those astray. (Al-Baqarah 2:198).

It is *sunnah* to spend the night within the boundaries of Muzdalifa; to perform the Morning Prayer as soon as the dawn breaks; to be engaged in reciting *talbiya*, *takbirs*, *dhikr*, supplications, and repentance; to continue the standing (*wuquf*) until first daylight appears; and to move towards Mina before sun rises.

## Performing the evening and night prayers together

In the evening of the Day of Arafat, it is necessary (*wajib*) for pilgrims to perform evening and night prayers together at Muzdalifa during the time of the night prayer. This prayer can be performed either in congregation or individually.

As long as there is no doubt about missing the night prayer, evening and night prayers are not performed in Arafat or on the way to Muzdalifa.

It is reprehensible to perform any other prayer, such as the *sunnah* or supererogatory prayers, between the two *fard* prayers. Thus, the *sunnah* of the evening and the first *sunnah* of the night prayer are not performed during the joining of the two prayer times. The two prayers are performed with one call for prayer (*adhan*) and one *iqama*. Another separate *adhan* or *iqama* is not read for the night prayer.

## The Stoning of Satan (*Ram al-Jimar*)

*Ram al-jimar* means that pilgrims stone Satan on the days of Eid. In Mina, where the stoning takes place, only the *Aqaba Jamra* is stoned on the first day; on other days, the small pillar, the middle pillar, and the *Aqaba Jamra* are stoned, in that order, with small pebbles that have been prepared earlier.

It is necessary (*wajib*) to throw pebbles at the *jamras* that are represented by stone pillars which are publicly known as the "small Satan," the "middle Satan" and the "big Satan." According to the general view, on the days that Satan is stoned, it is *sunnah* to spend the night in Mina; according to another view, however, for those who have

no excuse, to spend most of these nights in Mina is necessary (*wajib*). Mina is the region situated between Muzdalifa and Mecca, within the boundaries of the *Haram*
region, where Satan is stoned and sacrifices are offered.

## What are the conditions of validity for stoning Satan?

The conditions listed below are required for attaining a
valid stoning:

- Stones must be thrown at the *jamras* by hand.
  Throwing pebbles with a tool other than the hand,
  or just placing them over the *jamras*, is not regarded as a valid stoning act.
- Pebbles should be made of a material that is suitable for having dry ablution (*tayammum*), like
  rocks, hardened mud, etc. Stoning with pieces of
  wood, metal or animal droppings is not valid.
- Each of the pebbles must be thrown separately,
  one-by-one. If all the stones are thrown at once,
  it is deemed that only one pebble has been thrown.
- Pebbles must be thrown at the proper stoning
  place, which is the stone pillar and the pool surrounding this pillar. Pebbles that did not reach
  their targets are not counted as valid.
- Thrown pebbles must reach their target as a result
  of the effort of the person who threw it. If the
  thrown pebble falls into the proper place after
  hitting somewhere, it is regarded as valid; but if

it reaches its target with the interference of another person, then this pebble is not regarded as valid and it should, therefore, be re-thrown.

- Those who have enough power must throw the pebbles themselves. For a person to be eligible to select somebody as his/her representative in the throwing of the pebbles, he or she has to be in a very weak situation where he or she cannot perform prayers standing up.

- It is essential to throw the pebbles at the appointed times.

## When does the stoning of Satan take place?

Stoning days begin with the dawn of the first day of the Eid and continue until the sunset of the fourth day of the Eid. There are, however, some times in which stoning is not allowed. Let us now consider the stoning times one-by-one.

### a. The first day of the Eid (10ᵗʰ of Dhu al-Hijja)

On this day, only seven pebbles are thrown at the *Aqaba Jamra*. Stoning on the first day begins as the first dawn breaks and continues until the dawn of the next morning. Within this period of time, to throw pebbles before sunrise is reprehensible (*makruh*); to throw pebbles within the period of time between the sunrise until midday is *sunnah*, to throw pebbles from midday until the sunset is allowed (*jaiz*); and to leave stoning to after sunset, without any justified excuse, is reprehensible though permissible. Leaving stoning too late is regarded as *makruh*, because pebbles thrown in the dark may not reach their target and they may cause some harm to others.

Today, however, since there is enough lighting around the stoning area, this *makruh* is now invalidated. Moreover, as there is too much crowding during the day, and the lit concourse allows delaying, there is no objection today against stoning at night.

### b. The second and third days of the Eid
### (11ᵗʰ and 12ᵗʰ of Dhu al-Hijja)

On the second and third days of the Eid, seven pebbles are thrown at each of the three *jamras*. Stoning on these days begins at sunset and continues until dawn of the following day. It is not allowed to throw pebbles before sunset on either of these two days.

### c. The fourth day of the Eid (13ᵗʰ of Dhu al-Hijja)

According to Abu Hanifa, stoning on the fourth day begins at dawn. During this period of time, stoning before sunrise is considered reprehensible (*makruh*); stoning from sunrise until the *zawal* time (soon after the midday) is allowed; and stoning after the noon (*zawal*) time is *sunnah*. When sun sets on the fourth day of the Eid, the time for all stoning duties (both those fulfilled on time and those made up at a later time) is deemed to be finished.

## Can a representative be appointed for stoning Satan?

A person who is not able to throw stones because of illness, old age or a disability, should appoint a suitable person who will throw pebbles on his or her behalf. The criterion for a valid excuse regarding not throwing pebbles oneself is that of being unable to perform the daily prayers standing up. Those who cannot easily throw pebbles during the day simply due to the immense crowds, can wait for quieter times at night and can then perform their stoning duties.

It is not allowed for those who are able to throw pebbles themselves to appoint somebody else as a representative. For the appointment of a representative to be valid, weakness and impotence must be proven.

Appointed representatives first throw their own pebbles, and then throw the pebbles belonging to the person they represent.

## How can a missed stoning be made up?

Stoning that has not been performed at its proper time is fulfilled at other times within the stoning times. To fulfill the late stoning is necessary (*wajib*). The stoning time ends with the sunset on the fourth day of the Eid. After this time, neither stoning on time, nor late performance of a stoning, may be completed. It is also reprehensible (*makruh*) to throw more than the recommended number of pebbles.

## Shaving Off or Shortening the Hair

Shaving off or shortening hair is also among the necessary (*wajib*) hajj rites within the time of hajj or umra, as attested in the following verse:

ثُمَّ لْيَقْضُوا تَفَثَهُمْ وَلْيُوفُوا نُذُورَهُمْ وَلْيَطَّوَّفُوا بِالْبَيْتِ الْعَتِيقِ

Thereafter, let them tidy themselves up (by having their hair cut, removing their ihram, taking a bath, and clipping their nails, etc.) and fulfill the vows (if they have made any, and complete other acts of the Pilgrimage), and go round the Most Ancient, Honorable House in devotion. (Al-Hajj 22:29).

Anas ibn Malik, may Allah be pleased with him, narrates, "Allah's Messenger came to Mina and went to stone Satan, then returned back to his station in Mina and offered a sacrifice. After this, he told the barber, 'shave my hair,' and he pointed to his right side first and then his left side. And he presented his blessed hairs to people around who were awaiting."[103]

### When is hair cutting performed?

According to Abu Hanifa, the time of shaving or shortening the hair is all the days of the Eid, and the place of hair cutting is the *Haram* region. According to Abu Han-

---

[103] Muslim, Hajj, 86, Fadail, 75.

ifa, those who have not shaved or shortened the hair on Eid days, or those who shaved or shortened the hair outside the *Haram* region, must sacrifice a sheep or a goat because Allah's Messenger had his hair shortened in the *Haram* region, within the Eid days. Therefore, as delaying this duty is considered to be delaying a necessity (*wajib*), and since not performing a *wajib* act during the hajj requires offering a sacrifice as expiation, then sacrificing is applied upon those who do not perform this duty on time and in the appointed region.

A person who shaves or has the hair clipped at any time after the dawn breaks on the first day of the Eid has effectively come out of *ihram*. However, he or she will remain in the state of *ihram* within the Eid days as long as he or she does not shave or have his or her hair clipped.

The amount of hair which must be shaved or shortened is the same amount as that which would normally be wiped with the wet palm during taking ablution, that is, at least one fourth of the total hair. If there is hair on only one fourth or less of the head, it is then necessary to shave or shorten all the hair. Disregarding the amount of hair, shaving off or shortening the hair is *sunnah*. According to the Shafii School, to fulfill the necessity (*wajib*) duty, it is adequate to shave or shorten only three hairs from the head. Shaving off the hair is considered more virtuous for men than shortening it. Women, on the other hand, should shorten at least one fourth of their hair. It is reprehensible (*makruh*) for women to shave off their hair. The length to be shortened from the hair of a woman must not be any shorter than the tip of her finger.

## The order of hair cutting among the other rites of hajj

During the Farewell Hajj, when our Blessed Prophet came to Mina from Muzdalifa on the first day of the Eid, he first threw seven pebbles at the *Aqaba Jamra*. Then he offered his sacrificial animals and subsequently had his hair cut. Following this, he went to Mecca to perform his "*tawaf* of visiting," and then returned back to Mina.

There are differing views among Islamic scholars on performing hajj rites in this order, as Allah's Messenger performed it. According to Abu Hanifa, during the *hajj tamattu* (combining the hajj and umra with a break in between) and the *hajj qiran* (combining the umra and hajj in one state of *ihram*), it is necessary (*wajib*) to stone Satan, offer a sacrifice, and shave or shorten the hair, chronologically speaking; however, during a *hajj ifrad* (the hajj only), it is necessary (*wajib*) to stone Satan before shaving or shortening the hair. If pilgrim does not obey this sequence, he will be subject to an expiation.

According to Imam Abu Yusuf, Imam Muhammad, and some other scholars, on the other hand, to obey this sequence is *sunnah*. Although disobeying the sequence is reprehensible (*makruh*), if it is not obeyed, expiation is not required.

When the hajj is performed according to the clarification provided by Abu Hanifa, and this sequence is obeyed, those who have completed a *hajj ifrad*, after throwing pebbles at *Aqaba Jamra*, and those who have completed a *hajj tamattu* or *hajj qiran*, after throwing pebbles at the *Aqaba Jamra* and having sacrificed their animals, have their hair shaved or cut and come out of *ihram*. Those who will shave or shorten their hair in order to come out of *ihram* can either shave or cut their hair themselves, or have somebody else do it. All pilgrims are bound by the hajj prohibitions until they shave or cut their hair.

## What is the importance of shaving or shortening the hair?

Those who have their hair shaved or cut are regarded as coming out of their state of *ihram*. Coming out of *ihram* allows the wearing of normal clothes, the application of perfume, and the end of *ihram* prohibitions, like that against cutting the beard or moustache. Ending the prohibitions of *ihram* is called "*tahallul*." *Tahallul* occurs in two sessions. The repeal of all prohibitions other than the ban on sexual intercourse is called "the first *tahallul*," while the repeal of the prohibition on sexual intercourse is called "the second *tahallul*."

### a. The first *tahallul*

As *tahallul* means the end of the restrictions required by the state of *ihram*, the first *tahallul*—which repeals all *ihram* prohibitions apart from that on sexual intercourse—occurs when the hair is shaved or shortened. Hence, a pilgrim cannot come out of *ihram* by stoning the *Aqaba Jamra*, sacrificing an animal, or even by completing the circumambulation of the Ka'ba, if he or she did not shave or cut his or her hair. However, a pilgrim who had a shave or hair cut without doing these duties (stoning Satan and sacrificing) has effectively come out of *ihram*, and for him, all *ihram* prohibitions other than sexual intercourse are repealed. However, none of the restrictions for the first or the second *tahallul* ends unless he shaves, even if he performs the "*tawaf* of visiting."

### b. The second *tahallul*

With the second *tahallul*, pilgrims are released from all *ihram* prohibitions, including that against sexual intercourse. The second *tahallul* occurs when the "*tawaf* of visiting" is performed, after the first *tahallul* has already taken place.

### The "Farewell Tawaf"

The "farewell *tawaf*" is the last of the hajj rites. Performing the "farewell *tawaf*" before pilgrims return their homeland is necessary (*wajib*) for pilgrims who do not dwell within the boundaries of the *miqat* borders and who are regarded as *afaqis* since they have come to Mecca from a far distance. This *tawaf* is also called the "*tawaf of sadar*" ("the *tawaf* of leaving").

## What are the conditions of validity for the "farewell tawaf"?

In order for the "farewell *tawaf*" to be necessary (*wajib*) for a person, the following conditions must apply:

- The pilgrim must have completed the hajj duties.
- The pilgrim must be an *afaqi*. (The "farewell *tawaf*" is not obligatory for those who dwell within the boundaries of the *miqat* and the *Haram* region.)
- Women need to be purified from menstrual or postpartum bleeding. Those who commence menstruation before they perform the "farewell *tawaf*" and who will leave Mecca within the time of their monthly period are exempt from performing the "farewell *tawaf*."

## What is the time and the condition for the validity of the "farewell tawaf"?

The "farewell *tawaf*" is performed after completing the "*tawaf* of visiting," and its time does not end until one leaves Mecca and passes beyond the *miqat* borders.

Although it is more virtuous to conduct the "farewell *tawaf*" at a time close to leaving Mecca, it is also permissible to make the "farewell *tawaf*" at an earlier time. Those who performed it earlier do not need to make another "farewell *tawaf*" just before they leave Mecca. After completing the "farewell *tawaf*" there is no objection for those who would like to go to the *Haram ash-Sharif* to perform a prayer or supererogatory *tawaf*. In this case, the last completed *tawaf* becomes the "farewell *tawaf*."

## D. What Are the Sunnah Acts and Manners of the Hajj?

Apart from the obligations (*fard* acts) and necessities (*wajib* acts) of hajj, there are also highly recommended *sunnah* acts of hajj. Fulfilling the hajj duty with its *sunnah* acts will render a much greater reward and virtue. Further, it is considered reprehensible (*makruh*) not to conduct *sunnah* acts without any justifiable excuse. Although one loses a great reward by not practicing *sunnah* acts, however, one is not subject to an expiation for this omission.

Our Blessed Prophet personally exhibited how the hajj should be performed and said, "Learn your rituals (the hajj rites) from me, and perform them as I do."[104] Therefore, a complete, perfect hajj prayer can only be performed by practicing it according to the *sunnah*.

*Sunnah* acts of the hajj are listed in two groups as being either fundamental—those *sunnah* acts which should be practiced on their own—or secondary—those *sunnah* acts which are related to performing other obliga-

---

[104] Bukhari, Umra, 11; Hajj, 32; Muslim, Hajj, 154.

tory hajj rites. As the secondary *sunnah* acts of hajj have already been explained under the corresponding titles for the various obligatory hajj rites, we will now discuss the fundamental *sunnah* acts of the hajj.

## What Are the Fundamental Sunnah Acts of the Hajj ?

### a. The "Tawaf of Arrival"

To conduct the "*tawaf* of arrival" (the "*tawaf of qudum*") is *sunnah* for *afaqis* who come for the hajj from outside the borders of the *miqat* and who will perform a *hajj ifrad* or a *hajj qiran*.

There is no necessity to conduct a "*tawaf* of arrival" for those who are not *afaqis*; those who will only perform an umra or *hajj tamattu*; or those who will perform the *hajj ifrad* and will go on to Arafat without stopping in Mecca because of personal reasons, lack of time, and etc. The "*tawaf* of arrival" can be performed from the moment of arrival in Mecca until the time of the standing at Arafat. When the time of the standing at Arafat ends, the time of the "*tawaf* of arrival" also ends.

### b. Hajj Sermons

There are three sermons during the hajj: on the seventh day of Dhu al-Hijja, the first sermon is read before the noon prayer, in the *Haram ash-Sharif*; on the Day of Arafat (the eve of the Eid), soon after the noon time, before the noon and afternoon prayers are performed jointly at the *Namira Masjid*, the second sermon is read; and the third sermon is read on the second day of the Eid, before the noon prayer, at the *Masjid al-Hayf*, in Mina.

## c. Spending the night before the eve of the Eid in Mina

It is *sunnah* for pilgrims to set off towards Mina on the Day of *Tarwiya* (the eighth day of Dhu al-Hijja) after sunrise and to perform five daily prayers, from the noon prayer that day up to and including the morning prayer of the Day of Arafat, in Mina. After spending the night in Mina, it is again *sunnah* to proceed to Arafat, after sunrise on the Day of Arafat.

## d. Spending the night before the Eid in Muzdalifa

On the Day of Arafat, after sunset, it is *sunnah* for pilgrims to move from Arafat to Muzdalifa to spend the night in Muzdalifa, and then move towards Mina after the morning prayer, during the daylight.

## e. Staying in Mina on Eid days

To stay in Mina on the Eid days (that is, the 10th, 11th, and 12th days of Dhu al-Hijja), and to also spend the night there, is *sunnah* according to the general view, but necessary (*wajib*) according to some different views.

## f. Resting in Muhassab

Towards the end of the hajj, resting for a while on the way back from Mina in a valley called *Muhassab*, near *Jannat al-Mualla*, at the entrance of Mecca, is sunnah *al-kifaya* (the group *sunnah*). Since this valley remains within the boundaries of Mecca today, this *sunnah* can no longer be performed, and thus the pilgrims can no longer rest in here before entering Mecca.

## What Are the Manners of the Hajj?

We can briefly list the manners of the hajj as below:

- The hajj duty must be performed with financial means that have been gained through legal (*halal*) means.
- Those who have the right of others upon them must pay these rights back before they set off for the hajj.
- Sincere and resolute repentance must be made for one's sins.
- The prescribed prayers that have not been performed on time before must be made up as much as possible.
- Before going on the hajj, adequate information must be learnt from those who have experience.
- One must strongly abstain from ostentation, pretentiousness, or proud displays and attain a sincere, humble, and modest attitude.

- One should have fellow travelers (friends) with whom one can set up good relationships throughout the hajj.
- One should perform two *rak'ats* of prayer before leaving and after coming back home.
- One should pay farewell visits or calling on friends and relatives before going for the hajj journey.
- The pilgrim should abstain from all offensive and hard words and behaviors both during the journey to Mecca and during the whole hajj duty.
- Pilgrims should be careful not to waste any time on vain things and spend their time, instead, speaking words of adoration to Allah, through supplication, *dhikr*, *salawat* to Allah's Messenger, and the recitation of the Qur'an.

# What Is the Minor Pilgrimage?

## A. Description and Importance of Umra

Umra is a form of worship that is composed of entering into *ihram* without any restriction timewise (i.e. at any time of the year), and coming out of *ihram* after performing both the circumambulation of the Ka'ba and the *sa'y*, by shaving or shortening the hair.

According to the general view, for every Muslim who has attained the opportunity to make at least one umra visit to Mecca, it is *sunnah al-muakkada*. A different view suggests that it is compulsory (*fard*) upon every Muslim to make an umra visit at least once in a lifetime.

## B. The Obligations and Necessities of Umra

There are two obligations (*fard*) of umra: entering into *ihram* and performing the *tawaf*. Of these obligations, the state of *ihram* is considered a prerequisite (*shart*), and the *tawaf* is considered an essential (*rukn*). In turn, striding between Safa and Marwa and shaving or clipping the hair are among the *sunnah* acts of umra.

## C. The Time of Umra

There is no definite time appointed for umra. An umra visit can be performed at any time of the year. According to the Hanafi School, however, performing umra within the period of time from the Day of Arafat until the sunset on the fourth day of the Eid of Sacrifice is strongly reprehensible (*tahriman makruh*), while performing an umra visit within the month of Ramadan is considered a most virtuous deed.

## D. How to Carry Out Umra

An *afaqi* (someone coming from outside the *miqat* borders) enters into *ihram* correctly at the *miqat* border, while those who live within the *miqat* borders enter into *ihram* outside the *Haram* region and then perform two *rak'ats* of *ihram* prayer. After the prayer, an intention for umra is made with these words: "O my Allah! Only for Your acceptance and pleasure do I intend to make this umra. Please ease this umra for me and accept it from me." Afterwards, the *talbiya* of "*Labbayk Allahumma labbayk, Labbayk la sharika laka labbayk, Inna'l-hamda, wa'nni'mata laka wa'l-mulk, La sharika lak,*" is recited.

Then, upon reaching the *Haram ash-Sharif*, the intention for *tawaf* is made with these words: "O my Allah! Only for Your sake and for Your acceptance do I intend to perform the umra *tawaf*. Please ease this *tawaf* for me and accept it from me". Then the pilgrim strides between Safa and Marwa (going from Safa to Marwa four times, and coming back from Marwa to Safa three times). Following this, the umra visit is completed, and after the hair is either shaved off or shortened, the pilgrim comes out of *ihram*.

The difference between the umra and hajj prayer is that in the umra prayer, there are no rites to be performed in Arafat, Muzdalifa, or Mina; and there is no "*tawaf* of arrival" nor "farewell *tawaf*."

# How Many Types of the Hajj Are There?

## A. Types of the Hajj from the Aspect of Importance (Hukm)

With respect of religious importance, there are three types of the hajj: obligatory (*fard*), necessary (*wajib*), and supererogatory. It is compulsory for every Muslim who has financial facilities to fulfill the hajj duty once in a lifetime. To perform the hajj is necessary (*wajib*) for a person who has offered a vow to perform the hajj, although he or she was not liable to perform the hajj. It is also necessary (*wajib*) to make up (*qada*) a hajj worship that was interrupted for any reason after it began. Performing any hajj apart from either *fard* or *wajib* ones is considered supererogatory. A hajj performed by children who are too young to be obliged to perform the hajj, as well as the hajj prayers performed after the *fard* hajj of a person, is regarded as being supererogatory.

## An evaluation regarding the performance of the supererogatory hajj

Some people who have nothing to do with religion and never care about practicing religion assert that going for the hajj is nothing else than wasting money and causing a reduction in foreign exchange funds; perhaps, with these claims, they also influence some Muslims.

Yet the hajj is a command of Allah. No material assets can be compared with the values and merits that are gained by visiting these holy places, and there is no other means by which these values can be attained. Nothing can substitute for the obligatory hajj duty. What is more, the hajj is one of the five pillars upon which Islam is based. Abu Hanifa says, "I searched which act of worship is the most virtuous and after I went to the hajj, I understood that the hajj is the most virtuous act of worship among all." Because of this, those with adequate financial facilities should not be discouraged or prevented from going even for supererogatory hajj but should purify themselves by passing through this irreplaceable fountain of repentance. However, they can be advised to help their brothers and sisters in faith and provide financial support for students who are being educated for the service of humanity and for attaining a strong faith and deep knowledge of the Qur'an, and for the conduct of other good deeds which are rewarded highly.

## B. Types of the Hajj in Respect to the Way They Are Fulfilled

There are three types of the hajj in respect to the way they are performed. They are *hajj ifrad*, *hajj tamattu*, and *hajj qiran*.

### Hajj Ifrad

*Hajj ifrad* is the hajj that is performed without performing the umra. Since a pilgrim enters into *ihram* with the intention of performing the hajj alone, this type of hajj is called "*ifrad*," which means "a hajj worship without umra." Those who make intention only for the hajj, do not perform umra within the months of hajj, and fulfill all the rites of hajj are regarded as having performed *hajj ifrad*. Those who intend *hajj ifrad*, after completing all the rites of hajj, can still perform umra as many times as they like. Whether they are *afaqi* or dwellers from inside the *miqat* borders, everybody can perform a *hajj ifrad*. Those who perform *hajj ifrad* are not obliged to offer a sacrificial animal.

## Hajj Tamattu

*Tamattu* means "to gain benefit, or to enjoy the advantage of something." In this type of hajj, within the months of hajj in the same year, the intention is made separately for both umra and the hajj; their rites are fulfilled by entering into *ihram* separately.

Those who perform umra, come out of *ihram*, and then enter into *ihram* again in the same year, this time for the intention of performing the rites of the hajj, are regarded as performing the *hajj tamattu*.

This type of hajj is called "*tamattu*" (enjoyment), since there is a break between coming out of *ihram* after completing umra and entering into *ihram* to fulfill the hajj, during which the pilgrim is not bound by the restrictions of the state of *ihram*.

Those who would like to perform a *hajj tamattu* first enter into *ihram* with the intention of performing only the umra. After they complete the umra visit, they shave and come out of *ihram*. Then, when the Day of *Tarwiya* (the day before the Day of Arafat) comes, they enter into *ihram* again, this time with the intention of performing the hajj and fulfilling all hajj rites.

Offering a sacrificial animal in thanksgiving (*shukr*) is an obligation for those who perform *hajj tamattu*.

## Hajj Qiran

*Hajj qiran* means to join the umra and hajj prayers in the same *ihram* together during the hajj months of the same year. Since the hajj and umra are performed in one *ihram*, this type of hajj is called *qiran*, which means "to join." After making the intention for the combined umra and hajj, and completing the rites of umra, *afaqi* pilgrims who are coming to the hajj from outside the *Hill* and *Haram* regions perform a *hajj qiran* without coming out of the state of *ihram* which they entered into for umra.

Those who would like to perform a *hajj qiran* make the intention for both umra and hajj at the *miqat* border and enter into *ihram*. When they come to Mecca, they first perform umra and maintain the state of *ihram* until the days of hajj; and after they perform all the rites of hajj with the same *ihram*, they come out of the state of *ihram*. As is the case for *hajj tamattu*, those who perform a *hajj qiran* are also obliged to offer a sacrificial animal in thanksgiving (*shukr*).

## What are the conditions of hajj tamattu and hajj qiran?

- Pilgrims who will perform a *hajj tamattu* or *hajj qiran* must be *afaqi*. According to the general view, those who dwell in the regions of the *Haram* and the *Hill* regions, within the borders of the *miqat*, are not allowed to perform a *hajj tamattu* or *hajj qiran*. These people can only perform a *hajj ifrad*.
- Umra and hajj must be performed in the hajj months of the same year. If umra is performed before the *hajj* months have arrived, then this hajj is neither *hajj tamattu* nor *hajj qiran*, but is regarded as *hajj ifrad*.
- After the umra that is performed within the hajj months, the pilgrim must not return to his homeland or come out of the borders of the *miqat* after fulfilling the umra.

The order of virtuosity of these three types of hajj is as follows: *Hajj qiran*, *hajj tamattu*, and *hajj ifrad*.

No matter which of these hajj prayers one has performed, one is counted as having fulfilled the obligation of hajj. As in all other acts of worship, the real virtuosity that is considered significant is the sincerity, zeal, perseverance, modesty, and submission that is exhibited during the performance of this blessed worship.

# How Are the Hajj and Umra Performed?

## Preparation for Entering into the State of Ihram

The rites of hajj and umra begin by entering into *ihram*. Before entering into the state of *ihram*, general cleanliness of the body must be achieved, so that nails must be clipped; underarm and pubic hair must be removed; hair must be groomed; moustache and beard must be trimmed, if necessary; an ablution must be made; and, if possible, a bath should be taken.

After this general cleansing of the body, men take all of their clothes off and don the clothing of *ihram*, which is composed of two pieces of seamless cotton material called "*idhar*" and "*ridha*." Men must leave their head and feet uncovered. They are allowed to wear slippers provided that these expose the heels.

There is no restriction for women to wear any of their daily clothes, shoes, socks, and gloves. The clothes should be clean and loose. The head must be covered, but not the face.

If it is not a time of *karaha* (one of three periods of time during the day when it is forbidden to perform prayers), both men and women perform two *rak'ats* of prayers of *ihram*. After this, making the intention and reciting the *talbiya* of "*Labbayk Allahumma labbayk ...,*" they enter into the state of *ihram*.

Those who will perform a *hajj ifrad* make the intention only for the hajj by saying, "O my Allah, I would like to perform a hajj prayer offered only for Your pleasure. Please ease the hajj for me and accept it from me." In turn, those who will perform a *hajj tamattu* make the intention only for umra by saying, "O my Allah, I would like to perform an umra prayer offered only for Your pleasure. Please ease this umra for me and accept it from me," and then they start reciting the *talbiya*.

Those who will perform a *hajj qiran* make the intention for both umra and the hajj together by saying, "O my Allah, I would like to perform the umra and hajj prayer offered only for Your pleasure. Please ease this for me and accept it from me," and then they start reciting the *talbiya*.

After the intention is made and the *talbiya* is recited, pilgrims enter into *ihram* and, therefore, they then become subject to the *ihram* restrictions.

During the journey, until they reach the Ka'ba, pilgrims try to constantly read the *talbiyas*; the *takbirs* of "*Allahu akbar, Allahu akbar, La ilaha illa'llahu Allahu akbar, wa'llahu akbar wa li'llahi'l-hamd,*" ("Allah is the All-Great! Allah is the All-Great! There is no deity but Allah! Allah is the All-Great! For Him is all praise and gratitude!"); the *tahlils*; and the *salawat ash-sharifs* of "*Allahumma salli ala sayyidina Muhammadin an-nabiyyi'l ummiyyi wa ala alihi wa sahbihi wa sallim,*" ("O Allah! Bestow blessings and

peace upon our Master Muhammad, the Prophet who neither wrote nor read (any text), and upon his Family and
Companions!"). These supplications must be read at every
opportunity, especially when proceeding from one place
to the other, while climbing up hills and walking down
hills, when meeting with other *hajji* groups, and after
each prayer.

Repeating the *talbiya* three times at each reading,
then reading *takbir*, *tahlil* and *salawat ash-sharif*, is strongly recommended (*mustahab*). One ends reciting the *talbiya* when throwing pebbles at *Aqaba Jamra* on the first
day of the Eid, during the hajj, and when one reaches at
the door of *Haram ash-Sharif*, during umra; the *talbiya* is
not recited after this.

After being settled in a hotel or house in Mecca, pilgrims are recommended to take a bath, if possible, and
also to take an ablution for prayer; then they go to *Haram
ash-Sharif*, reciting the *talbiyas*. When the *Baytu'llah* is first
seen, three *takbirs* and *tahlils* are recited, and an invocation is expressed. If it is not the time for the prescribed
daily prayer, one starts to circumambulate the Ka'ba
straightaway.

## The Circumambulation of the Ka'ba

Since the circumambulation of the Ka'ba takes the place
of the *tahiyyat al-masjid* prayer (the prayer of greeting the
mosque) in the *Masjid al-Haram*, if a prescribed (*fard*)

prayer is not being performed, pilgrims begin performing the circumambulation.

The first circumambulation of the *hajj ifrad* is "the *tawaf* of arrival"; while it is "*umra tawaf*" for the *hajj tamattu* and *hajj qiran*.

Those who have entered into *ihram* with the intention of performing the *hajj ifrad* begin their circumambulation by expressing their intention with these words: "O my Allah, I would like to perform the "*tawaf* of arrival" only for Your pleasure. Please ease this umra for me and accept it from me." Then, on the way back from Arafat, if a pilgrim wants to perform the *sa'y* of hajj, which is supposed to be performed following the "*tawaf* of visiting", after the "*tawaf* of arrival," he should make "*idhtiba*" and "*raml*" during this circumambulation.

- *Idhtiba* involves putting the *ihram* cloth from underneath the right arm, leaving the right shoulder uncovered.

- *Raml* involves marching with a faster stride during the first three rounds of the circumambulation of the Ka'ba.

If a male pilgrim will not be performing the *sa'y* of *hajj* after the "*tawaf* of arrival," then he does not need to make *idhtiba* or *raml*. When the circumambulation of the Ka'ba is completed, two *rak'ats* of the *tawaf* prayer are performed behind the Station of Abraham, if there is a suitable place, or in another place, if there is too much of a crowd there. After making the *tawaf* supplication and drinking Zamzam water, those who perform a *hajj tamattu* or *hajj qiran* perform the *sa'y* of umra; and those who perform a *hajj ifrad* fulfill the *sa'y* of hajj, if they want to.

Those who perform a *hajj ifrad* do not come out of *ihram* by performing the *sa'y* of hajj and maintaining the state of *ihram*; instead, they wait for the days of hajj to come.

Since those who perform a *hajj tamattu* make the intention only to perform umra, they express their intention with these words: "O my Allah, I would like to perform an umra for Your pleasure. Please ease this umra for me and accept it from me." Then, they perform the *tawaf* of *umra*; offer two *rak'ats* of the prayer of *tawaf*; drink from Zamzam water; and go to Safa to begin the *sa'y* of umra. When the *sa'y* of umra is completed, they shave or cut their hair and come out of *ihram*. They then wait in Mecca without any *ihram* restrictions until the 8th day of Dhu al-Hijja, when they will re-enter into ihram, this time for the hajj. When the time for the hajj prayer comes, these pilgrims again enter into *ihram* and make their intention for the hajj. If they want, before they go to Arafat, together with a supererogatory circumambulation of the Ka'ba, they can also perform the *sa'y* of hajj, which they are supposed to perform after returning from Arafat.

Since those who perform the *hajj qiran*, while they enter into *ihram* at the *miqat* border, make the intention for the hajj together with that for umra, they express their intention with the following words: "O my Allah, I would like to perform an umra and a hajj prayer offered only for Your pleasure. Please ease this umra for me and accept it from me." Then they perform the *tawaf* of umra; offer two *rak'ats* of the prayer of *tawaf*; drink water from the Well of Zamzam; and go to the *mas'a* to fulfill the *sa'y* of umra. After they complete the *umra sa'y*, they do not shave their hair yet and they do not come out of *ihram*.

After having some rest, they can perform the "*tawaf* of arrival;" and after performing the prayer of *tawaf*, if they want, they can perform the *sa'y* of hajj. In the *hajj tamattu* and *hajj qiran*, since the *sa'y* is supposed to be conducted after the umra *tawaf*, pilgrims make *idhtiba* and *raml* in the first three rounds around the Ka'ba.

Whether they perform the *hajj qiran*, *hajj tamattu*, or *hajj ifrad*, all pilgrims must leave Mecca on the eighth day of Dhu al-Hijja and go to either Mina or Arafat.

## The Days on Which the Hajj Rites Are Performed

The hajj rites are fulfilled in six days between the eighth and the thirteenth days of Dhu al-Hijja. The rites that are performed in these days can be summarized as follows.

### a. The rites of the Day of Tarwiya (the 8ᵗʰ of Dhu al-Hijja)

After the Morning Prayer on the Day of *Tarwiya*, which is the day before the Day of Arafat, all pilgrims start moving towards Mina or Arafat. It is *sunnah* to perform the daily prayers starting from the noon prayer on the Day of *Tarwiya* up to and including the Morning Prayer on the Day of Arafat in Mina and, thus, to stay overnight in Mina and then proceed to Arafat after sunrise.

## b. The rites of the Day of Arafat (the 9<sup>th</sup> of Dhu al-Hijja)

Pilgrims continue to proceed to Arafat until the time of *zawal* (the time when the sun begins to decline soon after midday). After the noontime, if it is possible, a bath should be taken. Noon and afternoon prayers are combined and performed at the time for the noon prayer. After this, pilgrims stand for *wuquf*. They are occupied with reading *talbiyas*, *takbirs*, *tahlils*, *dhikr*, *tasbih*, *salawat ash-sharifs*, supplications, and repentance. After the sunset, before the evening prayer is performed, movement from Arafat to Muzdalifa begins. The evening prayer is performed just before the night prayer; that is, the evening prayer is delayed until the time of the night prayer, and these prayers are combined at the time of the night prayer. In the prayers that are jointly performed like this, the *fard* of the two prayers are performed one after the other and any *sunnah* prayer between the two fard prayers is not performed. In Muzdalifa also, pilgrims spend their time reciting *talbiya*, *tahlil*, *takbir*, supplications and repentance until the morning. Here, seventy pebbles are picked up to be used for stoning Satan.

## c. The rites of the first day of Eid (the 10th of Dhu al-Hijja)

When the first dawn breaks (the time of *imsaq*), the morning prayer is performed in Muzdalifa. After the morning prayer, pilgrims stand for the *wuquf* of Muzdalifa, during which prayers and supplications are expressed until it becomes very bright; then movement towards Mina begins before the sun rises.

After having settled down in tents in Mina, pilgrims go to the *Aqaba Jamra* to stone Satan. On the first day of the Eid, seven pebbles are thrown at the *Aqaba Jamra*. Each time a pebble is thrown, pilgrims recite, "*Bismillahi Allahu akbar, rajman lish'shaytani wa hizbihi*" ("In the Name of Allah, Who is the All-Great, I stone the cursed Satan and his party.") As the throwing of the pebbles starts, no more *talbiyas* are recited.

After stoning Satan, those who perform the *hajj tamattu* and *hajj qiran* offer the necessary (*wajib*) sacrifices within the *Haram* region themselves, or appoint a representative to slaughter the sacrificial animals. Those who perform the *hajj ifrad* are not required to offer a sacrifice, but if they want, they can sacrifice an animal as a supererogatory act. Coming out of *ihram* occurs for those who perform the *hajj ifrad* after throwing pebbles at *Aqaba Jamra*; and for those who perform the *hajj tamattu* and *hajj qiran*, after offering a sacrifice and shaving or shortening the hair.

If they can find the opportunity, pilgrims go to Mecca on the same day and perform the "*tawaf* of visiting." Those who did not perform the *sa'y* of hajj earlier fulfill it at this time. Performing the "*tawaf* of visiting" until the evening of the third day of the Eid is necessary (*wajib*) according to Abu Hanifa and *sunnah* according to other scholars. To perform the "*tawaf* of visiting" on the first day of the Eid is most virtuous.

After the "*tawaf* of visiting" is completed, it is a *sunnah* act to return to Mina and stay overnight there, according to the Hanafi School, and *wajib* according to the other three Schools.

### d. The rites of the second, third and fourth days of Eid (the 11th, 12th, 13th of Dhu al-Hijja)

After the time of *zawal* on the second and third days of the Eid, seven pebbles are thrown at each small, middle, and the *Aqaba* (big) *jamras*. Supplication is read after throwing pebbles at the small and middle *jamras*. As soon as the *Aqaba Jamra*, the biggest one, is stoned, the pilgrim leaves there at once without reading any supplication. It is to be noted, again, that the stoning of Satan is conducted not before the time of *zawal* but after it on these second and third days of the Eid.

On the fourth day of the Eid, those who will not stone Satan should leave Mina before the true dawn breaks (*fajr as-sadiq*). Those who have stayed in Mina for the fourth day must throw seven pebbles at each of the three *jamras* again. After throwing the pebbles, they go back to Mecca.

Before leaving Mecca, *afaqis* who come from far distances perform the "farewell *tawaf*." Thus, they complete all the rites of hajj.

## Female Pilgrims

Female pilgrims conduct all the rites of both umra and hajj, just as men do, apart from the issues listed below, and they obey all the rules exactly in the same way as men do:

1. While in the state of *ihram*, women may wear any garments like dresses, socks, closed shoes, and boots. Female pilgrims cover their heads but not their faces. However, they can still use a veil which does not touch their face. There are even scholars who think that this is highly suggested. Just as our blessed mother Aisha, may Allah be pleased with her, said: "While we were in the state of *ihram*, as we performed the hajj together with Allah's Messenger, when a mounted man was passing us by, we used to cover our faces by dropping down one end of our head garment (like a veil), and after the man passed by, we used to reveal our faces again."

2. Female pilgrims do not raise their voices loudly while reciting *talbiyas* or *takbirs*, or expressing supplications.

3.  They do not make *idhtiba* and *raml* while circum-ambulating the Ka'ba, nor do they make *harwala* during the *sa'y*.

4.  To come out of *ihram*, they do not shave off their hair; they only cut a little from the tip of their hair.

5.  If there are men around the *Hajar al-Aswad*, they do not approach it but rather just greet it from a distance.

6.  After performing the "*tawaf* of visiting," if they become ritually impure due to menstruation or childbirth and leave Mecca while the ritual impu-rity continues, they are no longer required to per-form the "farewell *tawaf*."

7.  During menstruation or postpartum bleeding, apart from the *tawaf*, they can perform all the rites of hajj. They will not be subject to any expi-ation if they wait for the bleeding to end and then perform the "*tawaf* of visiting" after the first three days of the Eid.

## Sacrificial Animals in the Hajj and Umra

### The sacrificial animals (hady) of the pilgrimage

A *hady* is an animal offered as a sacrifice during the pil-grimage. Thus, the sacrificial animals that are slaugh-tered in relation to the rites of hajj and umra are called "*hady*."

It is ordained in the Qur'an that,

فَمَن تَمَتَّعَ بِالْعُمْرَةِ إِلَى الْحَجِّ فَمَا اسْتَيْسَرَ مِنَ الْهَدْيِ

"...*whoever takes advantage of the umra before the Hajj must give a sacrificial offering he can afford....*" (al-Baqarah 2:196).

## The types of the sacrifices to be offered

Offering a sacrifice is necessary (*wajib*) for those who perform the *hajj tamattu* or *hajj qiran*. Those who perform the *hajj ifrad* or umra only do not have to offer any sacrifice, unless they are subject to an expiation. However, if they want, they can voluntarily sacrifice an animal. Sacrifices of *hady* are either necessary (*wajib*) or supererogatory (*nafila*).

### a. Supererogatory sacrifices

This is the sacrifice offered during the performance of the hajj or umra without any obligation, but simply to gain some reward. It is preferable for those who perform a *hajj ifrad* or only umra to offer a supererogatory sacrifice.

### b. Offering a sacrifice as a necessity (wajib)

- Offering a sacrifice for *hajj tamattu* or *hajj qiran:* This is the obligatory sacrifice that is to be offered by those who perform the *hajj tamattu* or *hajj qiran*, and it is considered to be an expression of thanksgiving for being able to perform both the hajj and umra.

- Offering a sacrifice in expiation: This is the sacrifice that is required to be offered as a result of either not performing or delaying any of the necessities (*wajib* acts) of the hajj or umra, or disobeying any one of the prohibitions peculiar to the *Haram* region.

- Offering a sacrifice as a result of an impediment (*ihsar*): This is the sacrifice that is required to be offered by those who come out of the state *ihram* after making the intention for hajj and umra and entering into *ihram*, but who are prevented from circumambulating around the Ka'ba and/or cannot stand at Arafat for any reason.

- Offering a sacrifice to fulfill a vow: This is the sacrifice that is offered in the *Haram* region to fulfill a vow. Offering such a sacrifice is considered to be a necessity (*wajib* act).

## The time and place of the sacrifice

No matter whether they are offered as a necessity (*wajib* act) or supererogatory act of worship, all the sacrifices (*hady*) are slaughtered within the boundaries of the *Haram* region. It is more virtuous to offer sacrifices that will be slaughtered until the evening of the third day of the Eid in Mina, and those that will be slaughtered on other days in Mecca.

The sacrifices of the *hajj tamattu* or *hajj qiran* can be slaughtered after the true dawn breaks (*fajr as-sadiq*) on the first day of the Eid, and it is not permitted to offer sacrifices before this time. Offering the sacrifices of the *hajj tamattu* or *hajj qiran* from the 1st, 2nd days of the Eid until the evening of the third day of the Eid is *wajib* according to Abu Hanifa, and *sunnah* according to Abu Yusuf and Imam Muhammad. According to Abu Hanifa, if the sacrifice is not offered on these days without any justified excuse, two sacrifices must later be offered, one of which will be for expiation.

## The meat of the sacrificial animals

Everybody can eat from the meat of animals that are slaughtered as thanksgiving (*shukr*) or supererogatory (*nafila*) sacrifices by those pilgrims who perform the *hajj tamattu* or *hajj qiran*. However, the meat of animals that are slaughtered in expiation for not performing or for delaying a hajj rite, as well as the meat of *ihsar* sacrifices, cannot be eaten by the people who offer these sacrificial animals, nor by their close relatives, nor by wealthy people. As is the case for the sacrifices offered to fulfill a vow, the meat of these animals must be distributed only to the poor and the destitute.

## *Fasting in place of sacrificing an animal*

Pilgrims who have intended the *hajj tamattu* or *hajj qiran* and who are, therefore, obliged to offer a sacrifice of thanksgiving (*shukr*), but cannot afford it or cannot find an opportunity to sacrifice an animal, must fast for a total of ten days. They fast for three days during the hajj, and the remaining seven days after the hajj. The first three days of this fasting, which must be performed during the hajj, must be fulfilled after getting into the state of *ihram* and before the days of the Eid of Sacrifice.

After having fasted for three days, and before shaving or cutting the hair on one of the Eid days, when a sacrifice can be offered, if the pilgrim suddenly finds the opportunity to complete the sacrifice, then he or she must fulfill the duty of offering the sacrifice because, essentially, the fasting cannot replace the sacrifice. But if the pilgrim obtains this opportunity after the days for offering the sacrifice during the Eid (the first three days of the Eid) have passed, then he or she does not need to offer a sacrifice.

Both the three days of fasting during the hajj and the seven days of fasting after the hajj need not be fasted consecutively; however, fasting these days without allowing any break in between is considered much more virtuous.

# What Are the Violations of Hajj and Umra?

Before we explain what the violations (*jinayat*) of the hajj and umra are, we had better first look at the meaning of the term "violation" (*jinaya*) in the context of hajj and umra, and the relative penances and forms of expiation.

## A. The Meaning of a "Violation" (*Jinaya*)

After making the intention to perform the hajj or umra and entering into the state of *ihram*, committing any of the acts which are prohibited while in the state of *ihram* is known as "*jinaya*." Further, failing to perform, or delaying, one of the necessary (*wajib*) rites of hajj or umra without any justifiable excuse is considered to be a penal offence (*jinaya*).

Note that the violations (*jinayat*) that are related to the *Haram* region or the prohibitions of *ihram* are absolutely subject to an expiation, regardless of whether the violation is committed with a justifiable excuse or not; whether the one committing the offence knew that this was a violation or not; whether the violation is committed by mistake or misguidance; and whether the violation is committed as a result of being asleep or forgetting. If these violations are committed knowingly (on purpose), atonement and serious repentance are also required.

## B. Penalties and the Expiation
## for the Violations (*Jinayat*)

While some of the violations committed during the performance of the hajj rites nullify the hajj entirely and necessitate the making-up (*qada*) of the hajj in another year, other violations require various penalties and expiation. We can list these penalties and expiation in respect to the violation committed as follows:

- *Qada*: This refers to violations requiring that the hajj be entirely made up. (See details under the next heading.)
- *Badana*: This refers to violations requiring the sacrifice of a cow or a camel.
- *Dam*: This refers to violations requiring the sacrifice of a sheep or a goat.
- *Sadaqa*: This refers to violations requiring the donation of alms in the amount of the *sadaqa of fitr*. (*Fitr* is the amount of alms given to a poor person during Ramadan, and which is equal to the amount normally spent by the benefactor for a typical meal.)
- *Tasadduq*: This refers to violations that require the donation of alms in an amount less than the *fitr*.
- Paying compensation
- *Sawm*: This refers to violations requiring certain days of fasting.

### Violations that nullify the Hajj or Umra and which require the pilgrim to make it up

After entering into *ihram* with the intention of performing the hajj, and before the standing at Arafat, if one has sexual relations, this nullifies the hajj prayer and requires that another hajj be fulfilled in the following years. Not only must the hajj duty be made up in later years, but a sheep or goat must also be sacrificed.

In the Qur'an, Allah the Almighty orders that,

$$\text{الْحَجُّ أَشْهُرٌ مَّعْلُومَاتٌ ۚ فَمَن فَرَضَ فِيهِنَّ الْحَجَّ فَلَا}$$

$$\text{رَفَثَ وَلَا فُسُوقَ وَلَا جِدَالَ فِي الْحَجِّ}$$

"*The Hajj is in the months well-known. Whoever undertakes that duty of Hajj in them, there is no sensual indulgence, nor wicked conduct, nor disputing during the Hajj*" (al-Baqarah 2:197), and has Allah thus prohibited all kinds of sensual indulgences during the hajj. If any sexual relations between the spouses happen after the standing at Arafat but before shaving or shortening the hair and coming out of the state of *ihram*, the hajj is not invalidated; however, a *badana* (cattle or camel) sacrifice must be offered as expiation.

### Violations that require sacrificing a badana (a cattle or camel)

1. Sexual intercourse after the standing at Arafat but before shaving or shortening the hair and coming out of *ihram*.

2. Performing the "*tawaf* of visiting" while one is in a state of rit ual impurity (*junub*).

It is necessary (*wajib*) to circumambulate the Ka'ba with ablution. The violation for performing the "*tawaf* of visiting" without ablution necessitates sacrificing a *dam* (sheep or goat). No matter the type of *tawaf*, if it has been performed without ablution or while in a state of ritual impurity, then it needs to be re-performed properly with ablution. There is no expiation required after the *tawaf* is made up.

## Violations that require sacrificing a dam (a sheep or goat)

These violations are listed in two groups as violations related to the necessities (*wajib* acts) of hajj and umra, and violations related to disobedience regarding *ihram* prohibitions.

### a. Violations related to not following the necessities (*wajib* acts) of hajj and umra

- Passing from the *miqat* border without *ihram*
- Not performing the whole, or at least four laps, of the striding between Safa and Marwa
- Not performing the standing at Muzdalifa without any justifiable excuse
- While stoning Satan, not throwing all or most of the pebbles that are supposed to be thrown in

one day within the specified time. (If more than half of the pebbles are thrown, charity (*sadaqa*) must be given for each of the missed pebbles.)

– Not performing the last three or only one round of the "*tawaf* of visiting," or the *umra tawaf*

– Not fulfilling the conditions of *satr al-awrat* (covering certain parts of the body) during the obligatory (*fard*) and necessary (*wajib*) *tawafs*

– Performing the "*tawaf* of visiting" or the *umra tawaf* without ablution; or performing the "*tawaf* of arrival" or the *umra tawaf* while in a state of ritual impurity (*junub*). If the *tawaf* is made up with an ablution, then expiation is not required. According to the Shafii, Hanbali, and Maliki Schools, cleanliness from ritual impurities is a condition for the validity of the *tawaf*, and the *tawaf* that is performed without ablution or while in a state of ritual impurity (*junub*) is not acceptable.

– Leaving Arafat on the Day of Arafat before sunset

– According to Abu Hanifa, delaying the "*tawaf* of visiting" until after the Eid and not obeying the sequence of rites, such as stoning the *Aqaba Jamra*, offering a sacrifice, and shaving or shortening the hair).

– For *afaqis*, not performing the whole or at least four rounds of the "farewell *tawaf*."

Those items listed above also constitute the necessities (*wajib* acts) of hajj and umra. In the case of not performing or delaying a necessity (*wajib* act) of hajj, sacrificing a *dam* (a sheep or a goat) is required.

### b. Violations that are related to *ihram* prohibitions

– Shaving at least one fourth of the hair or beard, or the whole of any other part of the body
– Clipping all the nails, or the nails of one hand or one foot
– Having intercourse after the first *tahallul* (after shaving or cutting the hair and coming out of *ihram*) but before performing the "*tawaf* of visiting"
– Conducting acts like kissing and caressing one's spouse with desire
– Doing any of the following, for a whole day or a whole night: for men, wearing any casual garment as a suit, socks, underwear, shoes that do not expose the heels, etc., or covering the head and face; and for women, covering the face. If men wear such garments less than a day or a night, or women wear veil less than a day or a night, giving alms (*sadaqa*) is considered adequate as expiation.

- Putting on perfume, oil, or styling gel on the hair or beard, or dyeing the hair or beard with henna, or putting any dye on them, all at once and in one place
- Putting on scents, perfumes, or oil on the whole or any limb of the body all at once, in one place

### Violations that require giving the alms of fitr

- Putting a scent or perfume only on a part of an organ (If the whole organ is scented with perfume, then a violation related to *ihram* prohibition is considered to have been committed.)
- Cutting some of the nails of a hand or a foot
- Wearing any garment for less than a day or less than a whole night
- Throwing an insufficient number of pebbles while stoning Satan (A separate penalty applies for each stone that is not thrown.)
- Not covering the *satr al-awrat* (defined parts of body) during the voluntary *tawafs*
- Conducting the "*tawaf* of arrival" or the "farewell *tawaf*" without ablution (while in need of ablution)
- Not performing the "farewell *tawaf*" or any laps after the fourth lap of the *sa'y* (For every missing lap, a penalty applies.)

## Violations that require giving alms less than the amount of fitr (tasadduq)

For a person who is in the state of *ihram*, violations that require giving only alms (*sadaqa*) include killing or taking and throwing a cricket, fly, or a flea that has landed on the body; or showing a flea that is on someone else so that the person can kill it.

People who conduct such acts while in the state of *ihram* should give alms (*sadaqa*) as much as they like. If the number of killed fleas is more than three, however, then alms in the amount of *fitr* must be given.

## Paying compensation

It is forbidden (*haram*) for everybody in the *Haram* region—whether they are in the state of *ihram* or not—to break off, pluck, pick or cut any tree, plant, or bush that is naturally grown in the *Haram* region, or to hunt any animal in this region. A person who harms the greenery or cuts or plucks off a tree or any plant that is naturally grown in the *Haram* region should estimate the value of this plant and give the amount of charity to the poor. If the plant is under the possession of someone in particular, then its value must be paid to the owner. If the killed animal is one whose meat is not consumable (like a lion), then the amount of the penalty cannot surpass the value of a sheep or a goat. However, if the killed animal is one whose meat is edible, then two just people must estimate the value of this animal in the place where it has been killed, and the same amount of money must be distributed to the poor as charity. If this estimated amount is less than the amount of *fitr*, then fasting for one day is adequate. If this value is equal to the price of a sacrificial animal, then the one who committed the violation is left with a choice among these two options: he can either distribute the defined amount of money to the poor so as each needy person will not receive money (or any other value) neither less nor more than the amount of *fitr*; or he can fast a number of days, each of which corresponds to the amount of one *fitr*. This fasting obligation can be fulfilled at different times.

If the animal is not killed but is, instead, injured or harmed, then the value difference between its healthy and injured condition is defined. If the harm done to the animal will not leave any sign or disability after it recovers, then there is no need to pay any compensation. If the killed animal is a trained animal, like a dog, then its whole real value is paid to its owner. If it is not trained, its value is distributed to the poor as charity.

One is not required to pay any compensation for taking only a few leaves from a tree grown in the *Haram* region so long as it does not cause any harm to the tree though it is also discouraged as one needs to respect the sanctity of the *Haram* region.

## *Violations related to not following the ihram prohibitions due to an excuse*

A penalty is applied to all violations of the *ihram* prohibitions, even if the pilgrim has a justifiable excuse. If the head of a pilgrim is shaved or the hair is cut prematurely, or he or she changes clothing, because of an unpredictable, unpreventable event, like being sick or having an accident, then sacrificing a *dam* (a sheep or a goat) is not necessarily required. A person faced with such an occurrence has an option of either fasting for three days at any time and any place; giving *fitr* charity to six poor people; or sacrificing a sheep or a goat in the *Haram* region at any time he or she wants.

## *The time and location of the compensation to be paid*

A specified time is not defined for the payment of the penalties related to violations committed during the hajj or umra. Although the penalty can be paid at any time during one's lifetime, accomplishing the compensation as soon as possible, in order to redress the violation conducted during the hajj or umra, is the most virtuous act. However, if the person who delayed the payment of a penalty dies before fulfilling this duty, then he or she is accountable for this violation and must provide for the payment of this penalty through his or her last will and testament.

A sacrifice that must be offered as a penalty for any violation must be slaughtered in the *Haram* region. The meat of such an animal can either be distributed to the poor living in the *Haram* region, or it can be sent to other parts of the world.

For the violations committed, a location is not defined in which to give alms, pay compensation, or fast. Those who committed the violations can execute these penalties anywhere they want.

## What do the Prevention (*Ihsar*) and the Omission of the Performance of the Hajj (*Fawat*) Mean?

### A. Prevention (*Ihsar*)

*Ihsar* means not being able to circumambulate around the Ka'ba and stand at Arafat for any reason after one makes the intention for the hajj or umra and enters into the state of *ihram*. If the pilgrim becomes able to perform any one of these two duties, then *ihsar* does not occur.

*Ihsar* happens when impediments—like an enemy blockade, the closure of roads due to war, severe financial straits, or the serious illness or death of the *mahram* accompanying a woman during the hajj—hinders a person from circumambulating around the Ka'ba and standing at Arafat. A person who entered into *ihram* can come out of *ihram* only after fulfilling the hajj or umra prayer. A person who is prevented from fulfilling the hajj or umra by such serious impediments comes out of *ihram* by offering a sacrificial animal for *ihsar* in the *Haram* region.

Hajj or umra prayers that cannot be completed due to any impediment must be made up at a later time.

## B. Missing the Performance of the Hajj (*Fawat*)

*Fawat* denotes the situation which occurs when a person who entered into *ihram* to perform the hajj is not able to reach the time for the standing at Arafat, even for a very short time, on the Day of Arafat. A person who cannot reach the Arafat region—with or without a justifiable excuse—from the time of noon on the Day of Arafat until the break of dawn on the Eid Day cannot complete the hajj and thus is considered to have missed the hajj of that year.

The person who misses the standing at Arafat must make up the hajj duty in later years.

# Is it Possible to Perform the Hajj on Behalf of Someone Else?

Acts of worship can be grouped into three as those performed physically, such as the daily prayers or the fasting; those fulfilled financially, such as almsgiving or offering a sacrifice; and those performed both physically and financially, like the hajj or umra.

One may perform an act of worship on behalf of somebody else and thus present its reward to that person. However, when people appoint somebody else to perform obligatory acts of worship on their behalf, are they free from the responsibility of fulfilling obligatory (*fard*) and necessary (*wajib*) acts of worship? For the acts of worship that are performed physically, like the prescribed daily prayers and fasting in month of Ramadan, appointing a proxy for one is definitely not allowed. Even if somebody else performs daily prayers or observes the fast in the month of Ramadan on one's behalf, the person will not be free from the responsibility.

However, for the acts of worship that are performed with wealth, like charity, the prescribed almsgiving (*zakat*), or offering a sacrifice, appointing a proxy to fulfill such acts of worship on one's behalf is absolutely allowed. As a person can give charity or the prescribed alms (*zakat*) in person, or slaughter the sacrificial animal himself or herself, then he or she can also fulfill these acts of worship through a representative.

As for the acts of worship that are performed physically and financially, only when the person who is liable to perform such acts of worship is not capable or too weak, or there is any other justifiable excuse not to be able to perform this prayer, then it is allowed for a proxy to perform the hajj on that person's behalf. Otherwise, it is not allowed.

The hajj duty performed by a proxy on behalf of a person who cannot perform the hajj because he or she has passed away while being responsible for the hajj, is very old, or is critically ill, is accepted as having been performed by that person himself or herself. Thus, those who are liable to perform the hajj and have not been able to go for the hajj because of such reasons must fulfill this duty through a proxy.

Those who are obliged to perform the hajj, do not perform this duty in their lifetime, and die without sending a proxy to the hajj, must have a will which provides for a proxy to go for the hajj on their behalf.

A hadith narrated by Abdullah ibn Abbas, may Allah be pleased with him, related to this subject enlightens the question about the performance of the hajj by proxy: "In the year of the Farewell Hajj, a woman from Khath'am came to Allah's Messenger and asked: 'O Allah's Messenger! The command of Allah to perform the duty of hajj upon His servants has become obligatory upon my father when he was too old to be able to sit up on a carriage. May I perform the hajj on his behalf?' Upon this Allah's Messenger replied, 'Yes.'"[105]

Thus, it is possible for a compulsory (*fard*) hajj duty to be fulfilled by a proxy, and this is accepted as if it had been performed by the person liable for the hajj duty.

---

[105] Bukhari, Hajj, 1,2; Muslim, Hajj, 7/3.

However, there are some conditions which apply to such circumstances, as described below:

- The person on behalf of whom the hajj will be performed must be continuously unable to go for the hajj for reasons like being too old, having an incurable illness, dying; or, if the person is a woman, not having close relative (*mahram*) available to accompany her during the hajj. If the person recovers from this inability and regains the opportunity to go for the hajj, then the hajj that has been performed by the proxy becomes a supererogatory hajj, and the person must perform the hajj himself or herself.

- Hajj must have become compulsory for the person on behalf of whom a proxy will perform the hajj prior to the hajj journey of the proxy.

- While entering into *ihram*, the proxy must make the intention to perform the hajj only for the person he or she is representing.

- The proxy must not demand any payment for this. Hajj is an act of worship, and all acts of worship and prayers should be performed only to seek the good pleasure of Allah.

- All expenses of the person who is sent to Mecca as a proxy must be paid by the one who sends the proxy.

- The person on behalf of whom the proxy goes for the hajj must have requested the proxy to perform the hajj in his or her place.
- The person who is sent as the proxy must perform the hajj in person.
- The proxy must obey all the requests of the person who sends him or her to Mecca and must perform the hajj duty in the way that the sender wishes. If the proxy performs a *hajj tamattu* while the sender wanted to perform the *hajj ifrad*, the proxy is regarded as having performed the hajj on behalf of himself or herself and must return the money of the hajj expenses to the sender.
- It is necessary to obey the requests of the person who made the will for the hajj duty to be performed on his or her behalf and defined the amount of money to be spent as well as the place from which the proxy will be sent.
- The proxy must not perform umra for himself or herself before completing all the hajj rites on behalf of the person who sent him or her as a proxy.

# Chapter 5
## Some FAQs Related to the Hajj Duty

## Can Children Go for the Hajj?

hildren who did not yet reach puberty can also go to Mecca and perform the hajj. This hajj prayer is regarded as a supererogatory hajj prayer for them. If children go to the hajj before they reach the age of puberty, in their adolescence, after they have become obligated to perform all prayers, and if they have an adequate level of financial resources to allow them to go for the hajj, then they must go to Mecca again to fulfill the hajj prayer.

During the time of our blessed Prophet, children also used to go for the hajj. We can recall this hadith of Allah's Messenger upon this subject: Ibn Abbas, may Allah be pleased with him, narrates; "Allah's Messenger came across a group of travelers in Rawha. Holding up a child, a woman from this group asked him: 'Is it allowed to perform the hajj for this one?' 'Yes, it is, and there is a reward for you from this,' replied Allah's Messenger."[106]

In another hadith, Saib ibn Yazid informs us that children were also performing the hajj during the time of Allah's Messenger: "My father made me to perform the hajj prayer together with Allah's Messenger during the Farewell Hajj. I was then seven years old."[107]

## Is Offering a Sacrifice an Obligatory Condition in Performing the Hajj?

If a pilgrim performs a hajj which is considered to be *qiran* (simultaneous hajj and umra) or *tamattu* (immediately consecutive hajj and umra), since Allah bestowed upon him to also perform umra together with the compulsory prayer of hajj, as a thanksgiving, he sacrifices an animal. A pilgrim who performs *hajj ifrad* (the hajj only, with no umra), however, does not have to fulfill the requirement of sacrificing. According to the Shafii School, *hajj ifrad* is more virtuous than the *hajj tamattu* and *hajj qiran*. *Hajj ifrad* is performed by not performing umra before climbing Arafat, intending the hajj only, and not coming out of *ihram* until the hajj prayer is fully completed. In *hajj qiran*, also, it is not allowed to come out of *ihram* until the end of the hajj prayer. In this

---

[106] Muslim, Hajj, 409; Abu Dawud, Manasik, 8.
[107] Bukhari, Jaza as-Sayd, 25; Tirmidhi, Hajj, 83, 925.

respect, those who do not want to perform a sacrifice make their intention for *hajj ifrad* and do not slaughter an animal as a sacrifice.

## Can the Sacrificial Animals of the Hajj Be Slaughtered in One's Homeland?

Is there a certain Islamic rule requiring that pilgrims must fulfill their sacrifices in Mecca? And if there is such a rule, what is the wisdom behind this rule?

Hajj is the term used for a prayer that includes visiting some certain places, during a certain period of time; obeying certain rules and manners, which consist of entering into the state of *ihram* with the intention of performing the hajj; standing at Arafat; and circumambulating the Ka'ba on certain days of the year.

A ritual that is required to be performed during the hajj cannot be fulfilled at any other place. For example, if a person, instead of climbing Arafat, climbs up another hill to perform *wuquf*, even if he performs days of *wuquf* on that hill, it will never be counted as it is from those who fulfill the obligatory *wuquf* prayer. Only if the *wuquf* is fulfilled on Arafat, where Allah commanded it to be, can it be acceptable as a proper *wuquf*. Again, the Muzdalifa *wuquf*, one of the fundamental principles of the hajj, must be performed by staying in Muzdalifa, the borders of which have been defined by Allah's Messenger.

Thus, as Allah defined how these acts of worship should be performed, He also defined the places where these services should be performed. As this is a matter of test through which human beings are examined, it is also a Divine command, the wisdom of which is kept hidden. Allah tests the submission of individuals through this sort of command.

Moreover, Allah purifies all sins from those servants of His who visit and stay in these sacred places. Since these places have interaction with the Divine world, they also have magnetic aspects. If those who enter in these places experience a tremendous amount of revolutions within their inner worlds, then the sacrifice itself, a service which has to be performed there, must also be fulfilled in these places.

The Ka'ba is blessed with such a sublime view of Allah's Benevolence that if a person will just sit by the Ka'ba, without even making *tawaf* around it, it would make Allah be pleased with him. There is such a strong and exalted Divine compassion on Arafat that Allah's Messenger gave the glad tidings that, except for only a little amount, all the sins of his community are forgiven on Arafat. And there is such a mysterious glamour in Muzdalifa that Abdullah ibn Abbas, may Allah be pleased with him, states that the rest of the sins that have not been shed on Arafat are all shed in Muzdalifa; he tells that this was the reason why Allah's Messenger smiled in Muzdalifa, but not on Arafat. All these places are so sacred and so completely filled with mercy and the blessings of Allah that individuals who go to these places gain an exceptional closeness to Allah. A special attribute is bestowed upon these places, as Allah has granted a special compliment to these unique locations.

As all these above-mentioned hajj prayers are performed in places that are showered with the mercy of Allah, sacrificing should also be performed within the boundaries of the Haram region. In performing sacrificing, which is an obligation on some pilgrims, to slaughter the sacrificial animal within the Haram region is also *wajib* (necessary). If a pilgrim does not want to fulfill this sacrificial duty, he or she can be free of this obligatory duty only by making the intention for *hajj ifrad*. However, if he or she intends *hajj tamattu* or *hajj qiran*, having a flame of enthusiasm to gain closeness to Allah, he or she will fulfill the duty of sacrifice in this place. Just as all services peculiar to the hajj are performed in those places, the thanksgiving (*shukr*) sacrifice must also be performed within the boundaries of the Haram region.

## Can Money to Be Spent on Buying a Sacrificial Animal Be Given as Charity Instead?

What would happen if thanksgiving sacrifices to be offered during the hajj were not ritually slaughtered as ordered and, instead, a pilgrim distributed the money to be spent on these to the poor of his or her own country? From time-to-time, such an idea is thrown out, though claiming such a thing is harmful in many respects. First of all, to make a decision originating in man and based only on human consent, leaving aside the command of the Book, can never be right. We should be, first and foremost, subject to the commands of the Book. Thus, it is not desirable to give the money to be spent on a sacrificial animal that is supposed to be slaughtered for the Eid of Sacrifice to the poor. The means of sacrificing is absolutely determined by a verse in *Sura al-Kawthar,* wherein the word *"wanhar,"* which is used to refer to the sacrifice itself, is a very specific word which requires "slaughtering a sacrifice by cutting the throat." Thus, the actual slaughter of the animal is required, while it does not make any difference if the person who sacrificed the animal eats all the meat or distributes all of its meat to those in need. And this is the point where charity towards the poor is advisable and desirable—in sharing the meat of the sacrifice once the fulfillment of the sacrifice itself has been completed.

In summary, if one's main concern is to help the poor, then this assistance must be provided separately, apart from fulfilling one's personal duties, those acts which are *wajib* (necessary.) Thinking about obeying the command of Allah by offering a sacrifice is a completely different kind of prayer than thinking about satisfying the needs of the poor and needy by being a generous kind of person. When the proper time comes, a Muslim will, in fact, fulfill all kinds of self-denying deeds that are expected of him or her. However, this is a separate subject than the present discussion. Where sacrificing an animal is concerned, we simply must know and accept that this is a matter defined and determined by Allah, and what is expected from us is to show respect to, and compliance with, this Divine order—regardless of any other supererogatory acts of charity or other duties we may engage in. For, being a faithful believer means submitting to the commands and prohibitions of Allah.

# Chapter 6
## Visiting the Tomb of the Messenger

## Visiting the Rawda at-Tahira of Our Beloved Prophet in Medina

After fulfilling all the hajj rites in Mecca al-Mukarrama and becoming a *hajji*, a pilgrim normally proceeds to Medina al-Munawwara and visits the *Masjid an-Nabawi*, the Mosque of the Prophet. This visit is not a part of the hajj rites. However, *Hujra as-Saadah*, the blessed place where Our beloved Prophet was interred is regarded as a very virtuous deed. For those having adequate financial facilities, making this visit following the hajj is seen as being nearly as important as a deed which is *wajib*, while not performing this visit without any valid excuse is regarded as great heedlessness.

Let us read together the hadith related to this subject:

- "For those who visit me after I pass away, it will be as if they visited me during my lifetime."[108]
- "Whoever visits me in Medina in full faith for gaining a reward, will be my neighbor. I will intercede (*shafa'a*) for them on the Day of Judgment."[109]
- "I will intercede (*shafa'a*) for those who visit my grave."[110]

Time to Leave

"For those who visit me after I pass away, it will be as if they visited me during my lifetime." Following this tradition, pilgrims visit the Prophet before they prepare for returning home, their luggage filled with love to share with others.

---

[108] Ali al-Qari, Sharh ash-Shifa, 2/149.
[109] Bayhaqi, Shuab al-Iman, 3/490.
[110] Ajluni, Kashf al-Hafa, 2/250.

- "It is not permissible to arrange special visits to any mosque on earth, apart from these three mosques; these are the *Masjid al-Haram*, *Masjid an-Nabi*, and *Masjid al-Aqsa*."[111]
- "A single prayer performed in this mosque of mine is a thousand times more virtuous (in respect to gaining reward) than prayers performed in any other mosques on earth, apart from the *Masjid al-Haram*."[112]
- "Between my house and my pulpit is a garden from the gardens of paradise."[113]
- "When any one of you greets me, Allah returns my soul to me. And I personally accept this greeting and reply the person."[114]

As it was compulsory to show respect and honor for Allah's Messenger during his lifetime on earth, paying respect and praising him after his departure from this life is also an obligation for us. For this, while visiting his tomb, one must keep away from all kinds of behaviors that do not comply with proper respect and high manner.

To go to the Quba Mosque on Saturday and perform there two or four rak'ats of prayer is a *sunnah* practice.

---

[111] Kamil Miras, Tecrid Tercemesi, 4/199.

[112] Muslim, Hajj, 510.

[113] Bukhari, Fazail al-Medina, 11, Muslim, Hajj, 502.

[114] Abu Dawud, Manasik, 96.

About this subject, Allah's Messenger said: "Whoever gets nicely cleaned and takes an ablution and then goes to the Quba Mosque, not for any other cause but just for performing prayers, he will gain the reward of performing an umra."[115]

## The Sanctity of Medina

Allah's Messenger declared the inviolability of Medina with this hadith: "O my Allah! Abraham is Your intimate friend and Your Prophet. Through his tongue, You proclaimed Mecca as sacred. O my Allah! I am also Your servant and Your Prophet. And I declare Medina sacred, with its place that remains between its two rock cliffs."[116]

## The Garden

The *Rawda* is the only building that can inspire us with the meaning and the spirit of being on this earth. Our relationship and heartfelt concerns related to this blessed building raise such sublime and sacred emotions in our inner worlds that while we reflect upon this building, and while we give tongue to our feelings about it, we greatly fear making even a tiny mistake, just as we feel when we describe the memory of a person known for his or her

---

[115] Nasai, Masajid, 9; Kamil Miras, Tecrid Tercemesi, 4/212.
[116] Ibrahim Canan, Hadis Ansiklopedisi, (Kutub as-Sitta), no. 6883.

pureness and chastity, who acquired monumental virtue and integrity due to a high morality, as we tremble with the feeling of a very deep respect. Every soul who passes through its illuminating ambiance can hear the echoes of this *na'at* (a poem in praise of the Messenger of Allah) by the poet, Nabi, and feel startled:

> *Sakın terk-i edebten, kûy-ı mahbûb-ı Hudâdır bu*
> *Nazargâh-ı İlâhidir, makâm-ı Mustafâ'dır bu.*

> (Abstain from any iniquity, for this is the post of the lover of Allah,
> this is the focal point of the Divine glance, and this is the Station of the blessed Prophet.)

The Ka'ba in Mecca, except during only a few short intervals, has been the niche of humanity throughout human history. And there is such a pulpit of this magnificent niche in the Mosque of the Prophet in Medina—may as many blessings and peace be upon Prophet Muhammad, the owner of this niche as the number of cells we have in our bodies—that is even purer than the gardens of Paradise: The *Rawda at-Tahira*.

*Rawda*, which means garden, in the interest felt by believing individuals towards holy things; with all of the incessantly changing emotions, thoughts and perceptions that emanate from this interest, is a sacred place which has always been circumambulated and tried to be bound with a rampart or a wall and which is indeed a garden of paradise beyond every imagination.

*Rawda at-Tahira* has many gates. The most meaningful of these gates is the *Bab as- Salam*, the Gate of Peace. Those who greet the Prophet while entering from this holy gate feel an emotional experience that is as if they are soon to meet the Prophet, the Master of All Hearts just two steps later.

Being subtly illuminated amongst the Allah-loving heroes of the heart who are performing prayers and expressing supplications and blessings to Allah's Messenger in great sedateness, gravity and equanimity, feeling themselves to be in the presence of the Prophet, and burning with the flame of enthusiasm at the same time, while proceeding towards the Encounter (*Muwajaha*, the fence in front of the tomb of the Prophet), a fully aware and alert person walks forward with a feeling at every step that he will suddenly be faced with surprises not imagined even in a dream. Then, the Encounter... Having reached there, pure and decent souls becomes blind to the rest of the world and what spills from their lips are praises for him, consoling themselves with his dream and good example. This is especially so if they arrived there with prior spiritual preparations; with previous experiences of emotional, conscientious depth; and with the infinite reach of their hearts, having laid their heads on that threshold in their dreams.

When one comes in front of the curtain from the direction of the *qibla* of this blessed resting place, one finds it resembles a face that smiles with sorrow and meets with hundreds of loving souls trembling with the excitement of hope and aspiration. This supremely green and charming climate of light grants everybody, according to their merit, the feeling of being in front of a gate to another realm. This is such an experience that every loving soul who reaches the Encounter feels so excited that they feel as if, a few steps later, they will meet the beloved and start to hear a composition which has never been formed or heard before. And, soon, sounds, expressions and visions of that golden climate will engulf them completely in a multitude of associations, taking them to a very mysterious zone that transcends time. Everybody who arrives in this zone perceives today within yesterday and apprehends yesterday within the "Age of Light" of our beloved Prophet, hearing the most intimate whispers that leak out from his conversations. And with a high level of excitement, they feel as if they will pass out.[117]

## Time Elapses As If in a Dream at the *Rawda at-Tahira*

Any part of life which is spent in proximity to the *Rawda at-Tahira* is experienced just like a dream or an imaginary world. Nearly every soul who has even a slight ten-

---

[117] Fethullah Gülen, Zamanin Altin Dilimi, 191.

dency towards Prophet Muhammad, peace and blessings be upon him, would never like to leave this magical atmosphere. Here, it seems as if all thoughts and ideas terminate, as all souls are drawn into the influence of their emotions and a strong desire to feel union with the beloved one besieges all hearts. Here, some intimate dreams that blossom in every visitor, like flowers, make their owners feel as if they can taste the pleasures of the gardens of paradise, and imbibe the tranquility and happiness of the dwellers of paradise.

We always feel ourselves being in a zone of worship at the Ka'ba, and in a zone of fervency, passion, and yearning at the *Rawda*. While we try to reply by comprehending the secret of servanthood at the Ka'ba, we embrace the latter with great sincerity and faithfulness. Even though we cannot exactly distinguish the essence of the things we feel here, we still perceive a world that is more emotive than even the most passionate of things; that is more exhilarating than even the most thrilling of things; and that enraptures us with all of its breadth, with its particular harmony, and with its special poetical atmosphere. Thus experiencing inexpressible feelings, we helplessly come into a position of full prostration.

Every time, this life that is lived between the tides of fervency and zeal is always experienced with a scent of union, a blessed joining, like the merging of a lover to the beloved. Every sigh and every whimper makes us shudder as if we are hearing the squeaks of the doors opening onto the beloved. It is as if all that is here—the walls, pillars and domes—has been carved by drills of affection, so that even the floor covers and the adorning cloths reflect the most subtle shades of blue, green, and yellow of the most delicate flowers, and are opened towards even the deepest beauties.

When the tomb of the Prophet and the Green Dome—which resemble a pure, decent, highly-esteemed soul in any case—come side-by-side with the deep worlds of the emotions and thoughts of ardent admirers, it gains such a deep enigma that one who experiences this thinks that the place being witnessed is simply a piece broken off from paradise.[118]

## Places to Visit in Medina al-Munawara

### Jannat al-Baqi (The Baqi Graveyard)

Situated on the eastern side of Masjid an-Nabawi, the Baqi Graveyard is a piece from paradise where rest more than ten thousand sublime guests—those who reached the highest level of humanity through being in the presence of Allah's Messenger and becoming his beloved Companions, some of whom left all their belongings and homes and made *hijra* (emigration); some of whom

---

[118] Fethullah Gülen, ibid., 194.

embraced warmly these emigrants, sharing all their sustenance and depicting an example of self-denial that has never been seen in the whole of humanity's history, either before or since; and all of whom showed the greatest altruism for the faith they believed in and, when necessary, along with surrendering their goods and possessions, were also willing to sacrifice their own lives.

So many exalted and revered members from the Companions and from the family of Allah's Messenger are resting here. The third Caliph, Uthman; the uncle of Allah's Messenger, Abbas; the wife of Allah's Messenger and the mother of all believers, Aisha; the beloved daughter of Allah's Messenger, Fatima; Sa'd ibn Abi Waqqas, a distinguished Companion who was announced by our Prophet as being among the dwellers of Paradise; the grandson of Allah's Messenger, Hasan; one of the four grand Imams of Islam, Imam Malik; and many more very distinguished members and heroes of the community of Islam, may Allah be pleased with them, are all present in this blessed place.

When visiting this spiritually rich graveyard, first those who rest here are greeted, and then visitors read *Sura Ikhlas* eleven times, and *Sura Fatiha* once. It is surely a highly virtuous act to present a *hatm* (recitation of the whole Qur'an) to the souls of these auspicious individuals, who sacrificed all of what was theirs for the establishment of Islam at the very beginning of this complete and perfect religion of Allah. There, visitors must at least read *Sura Yasin* and present it to these souls. Our beloved Prophet used to go to the Baqi Graveyard himself every so often and used to read supplications for the souls of his Companions in the Divine cause.

## The Martyrs of Uhud

Situated 5 km north of Medina, this blessed and tranquil place was once described by the Messenger of Allah as follows: "Uhud is surely a mountain that loves us, and we also love it, and it is based upon one garden from the gardens of paradise,"[119] where a very bitter struggle was conducted against the polytheists. In this severe battle, which happened in the third year of the *hijra* (625 CE), 70 Companions were martyred and Hamza, the uncle and foster brother of Allah's Messenger (since the mother of Hamza also breastfed the Prophet), the lord of all martyrs, was buried. The Messenger of Allah used to visit the martyrs of Uhud every year and used to offer supplications for them as well.

## The *Masjid al-Quba*

Situated at a distance of 5 km from Medina, the blessed Quba village and the Quba Mosque, which Allah's Messenger honored by his presence for 14 days during his

---

[119] Ibrahim Canan, ibid., no. 6884.

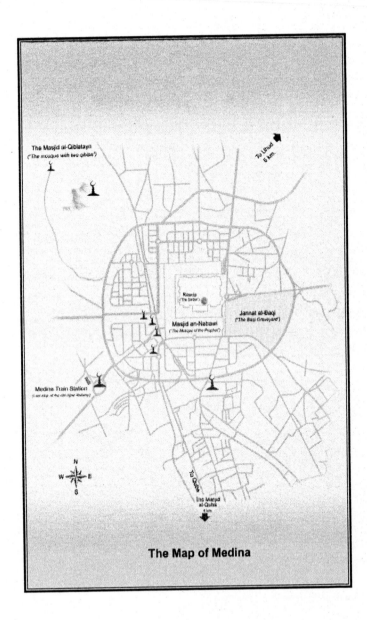

**The Map of Medina**

emigration from Mecca to Medina, built the first house of prayer, and lead the first congregational prayer, are praised in the Qur'an as الْمَسْجِدٌ أُسِّسَ عَلَى التَّقْوَىٰ "*being founded on piety and reverence for Allah*" (at-Tawbah 9:108).

To visit the Quba Mosque and perform there two or four rak'ats of prayer is regarded as a rewardable act. About visiting this mosque, our Blessed Messenger states: "Whoever, after cleansing himself properly and taking an ablution, comes to the Quba Mosque, for nothing else than just praying, he will gain the reward of performing an umra."[120]

Moreover, Abdullah ibn Umar informs us that: "Every Saturday, Allah's Messenger used to visit Quba Mosque mounted or by walking, and he used to perform there two rak'ats of prayer."[121]

## The *Masjid al-Qiblatayn* (The Mosque With Two Qiblas)

When Allah's Messenger came to Medina, he first went to his relatives—or uncles—among the Helpers. At the beginning—for about sixteen or seventeen months—he performed prayers by facing towards the *Bayt al-Maqdis*,

---

[120] Nasai, Masajid, 9, 2, 37.

[121] Bukhari, Fadl as-Salat, 3, 4; I'tisam, 16; Muslim, Hajj, 516, 1399; Muwatta, Salat fi's-Safar, 71, 1, 167; Nasai, Masajid, 9, 2, 37; Abu Dawud, Manasik, 99, 2040.

Jerusalem. His desire, however, was to face towards the Ka'ba, for which the instruction eventually came (al-Baqarah 2:143–144).

The first prayer that Allah's Messenger faced towards the Ka'ba was an afternoon prayer. A group from the Companions also joined Allah's Messenger for this prayer. After leaving this mosque, one Companion who joined this congregation came across another mosque. People in that mosque were performing prayer in congregation, and they were just at the bowing position. This Companion told them out loud: "I bear witness that we have prayed towards the Ka'ba together with Allah's Messenger." The congregation then turned towards the Ka'ba, remaining at their places and positions.[122] This mosque where the Prophet was ordered to turn his face towards the Ka'ba while leading the prayer in congregation was the Bani Kharisa Mosque, and it is still present today in Medina al-Munawwara under the name, *Masjid al-Qiblatayn.* When Muslims became a mature, exemplary community under the guidance of Allah to the right path, leadership was supposed to be taken from the children of Israel and be given to Islam thereafter. The changing *qibla* was an indication of this reality.

---

[122] Bukhari, Iman, 30; Baqarah, 12, 18, Salat, 31; Muslim, Masajid, 11, 525; Tirmidhi, Baqarah 2966; Salat, 252, 339.

The Blessed Messenger had already sensed this Divine intention and began to wait for it. This state of Allah's Messenger is so beautifully expressed in the following verse:

قَدْ نَرَىٰ تَقَلُّبَ وَجْهِكَ فِي السَّمَاءِ ۖ فَلَنُوَلِّيَنَّكَ قِبْلَةً تَرْضَاهَا ۚ فَوَلِّ وَجْهَكَ شَطْرَ الْمَسْجِدِ الْحَرَامِ ۚ وَحَيْثُ مَا كُنتُمْ فَوَلُّوا وُجُوهَكُمْ شَطْرَهُ ۗ وَإِنَّ الَّذِينَ أُوتُوا الْكِتَابَ لَيَعْلَمُونَ أَنَّهُ الْحَقُّ مِن رَّبِّهِمْ ۗ وَمَا اللَّهُ بِغَافِلٍ عَمَّا يَعْمَلُونَ

Certainly We have seen you (O Messenger) often turning your face to heaven (in expectation of a Revelation. Do not worry, for) We will surely turn you towards a direction that will please and satisfy you. (Now the time has come, so) turn your faces towards it wherever you are. Surely those who were given the Book (before, no matter if the hypocrites or the foolish among them deny or object to it) do know (the coming of this Prophet and this change of qibla) to be true (commandments) from their Lord. Allah is not unaware, nor unmindful, of whatever they do. (Al-Baqarah 2:144).

While visiting this house of prayer, what a beautiful feeling it is to remember this event that occurred fourteen hundred years ago and feel those days with a prayer of *tahiyyat al-masjid*.

# Chapter 7
# Hajj Memories

## Hajj Memories

I n this section we would like to mention some memories experienced during the hajj. We consider that delightful experiences lived while performing the hajj can provide useful inspiration for those who will go to the hajj, but we have only selected a few narratives from among the thousands of beautiful memories which pilgrims have expressed over the centuries.

## The Last Hajj of Abu Hanifa

The founder of the Hanafi School, and the great scholar of Islam, Abu Hanifa, whose real name was Numan ibn Sabit, lived in Qufa, early in the eighth century. It is narrated that this great Imam, who is generally renowned in the West for "being the man who established the methodology of jurisprudence and law," went on the hajj forty times. Each time he performed the circumambulations of the Ka'ba, rubbed his face on the *Multazama* and kissed the *Hajar al-Aswad*, and he exhibited his utmost respect in the presence of Allah's Messenger with a very deep enthusiasm.

During the days when he stayed in Medina, he always set up his tent one km away from the *Rawda at-Tahira*. In a profound and self-questioning manner, he acted like this because of his sensitivity and anxiety; "How can I go into the presence of Allah's Messenger? What if I demonstrate any improper behavior, or what if some unsuitable thoughts pass through my heart while I am there?"

Finally, he reached the age of seventy as he was performing his fortieth hajj. Again, he put up his tent one or two km away from the *Rawda at-Tahira*. As he stayed in his tent, he sometimes saw himself virtually in the presence of Allah's Messenger, and sometimes returned to himself. Some time later, he witnessed that a hand held the door of the tent. It was the hand of a bedouin who had, himself, just sat in the presence of the owner of the Green Dome only a few minutes ago, as the story explains.

For the bedouin was complaining about his poverty and family problems and was bellyaching like this: "O Allah's Messenger! I crossed over all the deserts and came to your presence; all things I have attempted have dried out, and now I have fallen into a situation where I cannot even keep my family's pot boiling. While I prefer you and your religion, on the one hand, the worldly things and worries are pulling me away!" While beseeching and crying like this, suddenly the bedouin experienced a different mood and witnessed the vision of Allah's Messenger. "Go now, in a tent so much further from here; there is a man called Numan ibn Faris. Tell him my greeting. And tell him that he can come to my presence now; let him come." And so ordered our Prophet to the bedouin.

While being captivated in his own deep feelings and sublime thoughts, Abu Hanifa saw the Bedouin, who had been so sorrowfully imploring at the Holy Shrine of Allah's Messenger, as he tried to open the door of his tent. As soon as the bedouin came inside, he humbly knelt down and told the Imam: "O Imam! The Messenger of Allah sends greetings to you. He has said, 'Forty years of yearning is enough'; and he has ordered you thus: 'Let him now come to my *Rawda*.'" The Grand Imam, Abu Hanifa, was very startled and told the bedouin: "Can you say again what you have just said?" And as soon as the bedouin repeated "Allah's Messenger sends his greetingto you," the Grand Imam took out all the money from his purse at once and gave them all to the bedouin and told him, "For the sake of Allah, can you please repeat that word you said?" When the bedouin repeated the greeting sent by Allah's Messenger, the Imam took off his precious cloak and gave it to the bedouin. And again, with great enthusiasm, "Can you repeat that word again?" he asked the bedouin. When the bedouin completed saying that, "Allah's Messenger sends greeting to you, 'Forty years of separation is enough, let him come to my *Rawda*,'" the grand Imam gave everything he possessed, including his clothes, to the bedouin. For the imam understood that this was an invitation, a very precious, expensive invitation. This invitation was, of course, a beckoning to go to yonder worlds, and it announced death as a very sweet passage to a reunion with his deeply beloved master in the eternal life.

Despite the blessing of this unique invitation, the Grand Imam remained in great modesty and propriety throughout the rest of his life, and always carried the worry of losing this manner because of the familiarity that this visit might have gained over time. When he was asked, "Why do you not live in Medina?" He answered, "I prefer to live in Qufa and carry the love and yearning of Medina in my heart. I would not desire at all to live in Medina and carry the love of Qufa in my heart. I fear thinking about, and missing, my children and family while walking on the streets of Medina. Because I fear this, I do not stay in Medina, for I cannot trust my heart, and I do not have enough courage to stay there."

By speaking like this, the Grand Imam perhaps wanted to remind us that those blessed places are not for staying permanently, but they are places to visit to be recharged; and after being filled with sublime feelings there, we must spread these feelings and experiences to different parts of the world.[123]

## Yearning of Said Nursi for Performing the Hajj

Said Nursi, the great Islamic scholar of the 19th and 20th century, did not go for the hajj during his entire lifetime. Despite his great ambition to go for the hajj, he could not. Particular socio-political conditions which prevailed during his life forced him to stay in his country and strive, with all his might, for the cause of Islam and the Qur'an, especially to try to save the faith of coming generations, who were broaching the danger of atheism: "In the eighty or so long years of my lifetime, I did not taste anything from worldly pleasures. My total life passed either in battle fields, or in my country's prisons, or in exile. There is not an anguish, nor a torment left, that I did not taste..."

These sentences summarize all his life's experiences. It was impossible for him to go for the hajj under these circumstances. In a letter which he sent to one of his students, we see that he was deeply longing for even some of his students to go for the hajj:

> If we would be free, at least some of us would have gone for the hajj. By the will of Allah, this intention

---

[123] Fethullah Gülen, The Sermons on Hajj, 1978.

of ours will be accepted just as we actually went to the hajj, and this service of ours for spreading the light of faith under these very stressful conditions will yield a reward as big as a reward gained from performing the hajj.[124]

Again, in another letter he wrote to one of his students, we see that he took a promise from him to perform the hajj on his behalf and tried to satisfy, at least somewhat, his unbearable yearning to go for the hajj:

We decided to make those blessed brothers of ours who went for the hajj from Isparta and promised to perform the hajj also on my behalf as partners to all our spiritual gains in the hereafter, who are counted within our intimate circle of sincere brothers. May Allah make them prosper both in this world and in the hereafter. Amin.[125]

The following words also belong to Said Nursi. These expressions show that Said Nursi was a person with a high mission who sacrificed everything in order to achieve his mission—leaving everything worldly aside, and locking on to realizing his mission. At any rate, the life he lived is also clear proof of this:

[124] Said Nursi, Şualar, (The Rays Collection) in Risale-i Nur Collection, p.1089.

[125] Said Nursi, Emirdağ Lahikası in Risale-i Nur Collection, p.1.

- "Serving in the way of the Qur'an is put over my shoulders as a Divine favor from Allah."
- "In my eye, there is neither any appeal for paradise, nor any fear from hellfire. If I will see the faith of my nation is saved, I accede to burn in the flames of hellfire."

Together with tremendous amount of effort he spent for his written works to spread all around the world, he regarded the fact that his compiled work, titled *Risale-i Nur*, was accepted in *Rawda at-Tahira* as a sign of the consent and pleasure of our beloved Prophet for this service:

Yes, as reported by those who went for the hajj this year, just as the translating and publishing works of the strong texts of Nur, both into the Arabic and in Urdu languages, have received great acceptance in Mecca al-Mukarrama, the Risale-i Nur Collection has been so much welcomed in Medina al-Munawwara that it was put on *Rawda at-Tahira*, the blessed tomb of Our Prophet. Hajji Sayyid himself saw that Asa-yi Musa ("the Staff of Moses," which is a book in the Risale-i Nur Collection) was on the blessed tomb of Allah's Messenger. This implies that the Prophet is contented with the Risale-i Nur Collection and it entered into the shrine of satisfaction of Muhammad, peace and blessings be upon him. As we intended, and as we said, the pilgrims who went from here have witnessed that the Nur Collection has visited those blessed places on our behalf.[126]

## "If I Knew, I Would Meet You"

Abdurrahman Cerrahoğlu, from Burdur, a student of Said Nursi's and one of the publishers of the *Risale-i Nur* Collection narrates the following:

"I intended to go for the hajj in 1954. I wanted to go to the hajj from Burdur. However, the police was keeping me under constant observation. Two days before I left Burdur, a policeman came to my house to give me a formal letter informing me that I was being called by the investigating magistrate. All I feared was that they would delay me fulfilling my obligatory duty of the hajj. I intended to go together with my mother and my wife. At once, I found Brother Abdullah Arığ, who was then a judge of the High Criminal Court. I explained my situation to him, and he told me: "Do not worry. I will come forward as a surety, and I can send you there.' And '*Insha Allah* we can meet in Jiddah,' he added. Apparently, he also intended to go for his first hajj. And indeed, although I went from Burdur much earlier than him, we did meet in Jiddah on the way back from Medina al-Munawwara. This indicat-

---

[126] Said Nursi, Şualar, (The Rays Collection) in Risale-i Nur Collection, p.1074.

ed the level of sincerity of this brother. May Allah bestow His Mercy upon him...

"Then, in 1954, we met the honorable Ali Ulvi Kurucu in Medina al-Munawwara. There, he introduced me to Hasan Hojaefendi, who was once the *mufti* of Van city. I found out that this respected man had always looked for somebody who personally knew Said Nursi. So the calligrapher took us to the workshop of Abdullah Efendi, who was originally from Konya. We sat there for a while. He asked many questions about Said Nursi, and he told me to convey his greetings and deep respects to Said Nursi. He also told that he was now married and settled in Medina al-Munawwara himself, and he invited Said Nursi there. 'Insha Allah, I will tell him all this when I go back,' I told him. He was absolutely delighted.

"So after I completed my duty of hajj, I returned to Burdur. In those days, Said Nursi was in Isparta, so I went there to visit him. He was seriously ill, and he was not able to speak clearly. He was saying some things, but we were not able to understand them. Brother Zübeyir, who was just by our *Ustad* (master teacher), conveyed his speeches to us. I felt deeply upset. At one time, when I mentioned that I went for the hajj and brought the greeting of Hasan Hojaefendi, who was one of Van's *muftis*, our *Ustad*, who was, up to this point, lying down like a dead man, suddenly sat up and asked 'What! Did you see him?' with excitement.

"Allah the Almighty granted that I saw him,' I replied. 'He told me that he is married there and that he is inviting you there,' I continued. '*Insha Allah*,' he responded. Then he asked many questions in detail. 'You went for the hajj, did you? May Allah make your prayer blessed and well-accepted. If I knew this, I would have met you,' expressed Said Nursi, and he continued: 'This greeting of yours has become cure for me. May Allah be pleased with you.'"[127]

## The Hajj Memories of Fethullah Gülen

*Rawda*, which is preferred over paradise, and its unforgettable memories...

In an interview held with Fethullah Gülen Hojaefendi, the widely respected contemporary scholar of Islam who first went for the hajj in 1968, he explains this first voyage to blessed places and its persistent influence over him, as follows:

"I first went for the hajj in 1968. I was then working in Kestanepazari, Izmir. When I saw the Ka'ba and the *Rawda at-Tahira* for the first time, I fell into such an emotional state that I could never describe it properly. And while it most likely would not have happened to me, if just at that moment, all the gates of paradise would have opened wide and I would have been invited inside, I

---

[127] Necmettin Şahiner, Son Şahitler, 1/234.

think that I would not have been able to leave there to go to paradise. To be present in the *Haram ash-Sharif* and the *Rawda at-Tahira* gave me such a high spiritual inward pleasure and delight. I always regarded my students in Kestanepazari in a very distinguished manner. I firmly believed that at least some part of the grand salvation of the world of Islam was being represented by them. While I was going for the hajj, I also took the list containing their names. There, I prayed for them one-by-one. Moreover, I mentioned the names of, and prayed for, many people whom I knew. In those days, the whole number of people whom I knew then, in and all around Turkey, was much less than today. Because of this, I was able to mention all their names. One of the memories that I could never forget regarding this first hajj duty of mine was as follows.

"In the *Haram ash-Sharif*, especially while the prayer was performed congregationally, watching the harmonious movements of the whole congregation, who looked just like a very colorful flower garden, incited me with really exceptional feelings and emotions. There, in their authentic clothes and garments, every single person having different colors was like a rare species of varicolored flower. And the *Haram ash-Sharif* was like a profoundly rich flower garden in which flowers bloom every season. Just to be able to see this view, I went down for *ruqu* (bowing down) and *sajda* (prostration) a bit later than others and I could not prevent myself from doing this.

"One day, I was on the second balcony to perform the Morning Prayer. I fulfilled the Morning Prayer with the same feelings, and I was busy reading supplications and in the remembrance of Holy Names of Allah. Suddenly, I could not see the owner of the voice, but I heard his voice all through my conscience. It was satan whispering evilly, 'Go on, throw yourself down from here!' 'What good is there in me throwing myself down here?' I asked. 'It does not matter, just throw yourself!' he replied. 'Alright, but why?' I persisted, trying to learn his intention. But he simply insisted, 'It will do no harm, go on—throw yourself from here!' Just in case, I stepped backwards. Just then I saw that Hacı Kemal, who was about fifty meters away from me, also stepped back. We were always together with him through the hajj, so later I told him what happened to me on that balcony. He told me, 'Oh my Hoja, at the same moment, I was faced with the same oppression, too. That was why I took a few steps back!' It meant that we both experienced the same state of mind at the same time and the signals from the devil were received by our souls just at the same moment.

"I was very determined that year that I was going to take presents to all my students and friends, no matter how big or small they were and I was going to definitely offer them Zamzam water. Allah granted me success in this intention of mine. I also gave one silver ring as gift to each of my students, and I gave dates and Zamzam to some of them. This was such a great, heart-warming event for me. I used to love my students so much..."

# The Final Word

Up to this point, we have tried to introduce the hajj prayer with its various aspects. Wishing a very blessed and most accepted hajj for those fortunate ones who will go to the hajj, we now would like to conclude our work with a compilation of highlights from this book.

- The hajj prayer, which is a right of Allah over everyone who is physically able and has sufficient financial means, reached us in its present form from Prophet Abraham. Also, being an intensive, collective prayer, the hajj is a worship at universal level for everyone.

- Allah bestowed sanctity over the Ka'ba, the *qibla* of people of faith. This fact is expressed in the Qur'an as follows: جَعَلَ اللهُ الْكَعْبَةَ الْبَيْتَ الْحَرَامَ قِيَامًا لِلنَّاسِ *"Allah has made the Ka'ba, the Sacred House, a standard and maintenance for the people (for both their religious and worldly lives)..."* (al-Maedah 5:97). The point where the Ka'ba is erected also offers a focal point of a grand meaning, for the Ka'ba is a niche where all the hearts of the faithful beat together, and it is a unique place of worship on earth which has been praised with the singular merit of being إِنَّ أَوَّلَ بَيْتٍ وُضِعَ لِلنَّاسِ "*the first House (of Prayer) established for humankind*" (Al Imran 3:96). Being the material cross-section of a radiant pillar from the centre of earth to the *Sidrat al-Muntaha*— around which human beings, jinns and angels always circumambulate—the Ka'ba is such an unmatched, sublime building that billions of visible and non-visible pure souls deeply long to reach its boundaries, and it can be said that its value is worth the whole of the created universe. It is already known, both on Earth and in the heavens, as *Bayt'ullah*, the House of Allah. And being the indicator of the beginning point of *tawaf*, the Hajar al-Aswad that is situated in one corner of the Ka'ba is a sacred stone upon which Allah's Messenger placed his blessed lips and cried for a very long time; and when he saw that Umar was also crying, he told him: "O Umar! This is the place where tears should be let to flow!"[128]

- Just as in each tiny memory cell of a human being, a tremendous amount of information and knowledge is saved, it can be said that Hajar al-

---

[128] Ibrahim Canan, Hadis Ansiklopedisi, (Kutub as-Sitta), no. 6852.

Aswad is also created by Allah as a kind of recorder of the times that saves all the moments of those who greet it, and it will become a kind of witness on the Day of Judgment.

- After making the intention for performing the hajj and getting into the state of ihram, the mountains, streams, stones and hills seem to become like separate tongues, all of which tell only one word: "*Labbayk Allahumma labbayk, Labbayk la sharika laka labbayk, Inna'l-hamda, wa'n-ni'mata laka wa'l-mulk, La sharika lak.*" ("Here I am, O Allah, at Your command! Here I am at Your command! You are without associate! Here I am at Your command! Yours are praise, grace and dominion! You are without associate.") The words of imploring which are uttered by all these tongues are the same; the affection and compassion in all eyes are the same; and the purity and lucidity of so many abounding feelings are the same—in effect, despite the diversity of color, race, culture, and language, the essence of what is experienced by each spirit is the same. In these sacred places and times, we carry on living the same things in different bodies, as though we were but one, single soul.

- For people of faith, the hajj is like a grand conference, a huge congress that is held once a year within the Islamic world. In the season of hajj, Muslims depart for Mecca from so many different parts of the world to fulfill their blessed hajj duties and to deepen their awareness of the global reach of their faith.

— We must hold fast to wisdom: "Employ haste in going for the hajj, for any one of you cannot know when the time of death will reach him."[129] While performing the hajj prayer, we must focus on gaining the consent and pleasure of Allah, Who commanded us to fulfill this worship, and we must always act with complete sincerity. Worship that is performed in consideration of some worldly benefits or interests can no longer be counted as pure worship.

— At the same time, the hajj is the best environment for blooming and strengthening in real kinship with one another. This is because, during the performance of the hajj prayer, people from all walks of life—from kings to drifters, from the rich to the poor, and from the palest to the darkest among us—all share the same simple garments, the same elevating atmosphere, and the same desert soil.

— There are glad tidings announced by our beloved Prophet in his saying, "Those who perform the

---

[129] Abu Dawud, Manasik, 5; Ibn Maja, Manasik, 1.

hajj and, and in the course of it, keep themselves away from intercourse, from speaking malicious words, and from performing indecent behaviors, will be purified from all sins, just like on the day they were born."[130]

– Our Exalted Lord Allah ordained the Well of Zamzam to be extracted for the sake of Prophet Abraham's prayer, Hagar's submission to Allah, and the innocence of the little baby Ishmael, so that it will bring life to Mecca. The story of Zamzam is like a well for our souls by which we may draw the water of faith.

– We are also inspired by the wisdom of the words, "Hajj is Arafat, and whoever reaches the Standing on the day of *Jam'*, that is, before the dawn of the night of Muzdalifa, it will be counted as having fulfilled the hajj prayer."[131] Arafat has such a deep spiritual atmosphere, and the time elapsed there has such a subtle depth, that every fortunate soul who has the chance of being there, even if it is only once, will never fall into complete devastation and will never die as other earthbound mortal beings.

---

[130] Bukhari, Mukhsar, 9, 10; Nasai, Hajj, 4; Ibn Maja, Manasik, 3; Darimi, Manasik, 7, Ibn Hanbal, II, 229, 410, 484, 494.

[131] Tirmidhi, Hajj, 57, 889; Abu Dawud, Manasik, 69, 1949; Nasai, Hajj, 211, 5, 264; Ibn Maja, Manasik, 37, 3015.

- Arafat is the place for expressing heartfelt emotions, for imploring Allah, and for unbounded adoration. On Arafat, a person testifies the most emotional and the most effusive supplications. Especially near the time of sunset, the supplications that are expressed with the sadness of the impending farewell are even more deeply felt—there, the noises and breaths reach such a subtlety and limpidity that they remind us of the screams and cries of angels living in worlds beyond.

- Muzdalifa remains the auspicious place where verdicts of acquittals are taken, and it is like a prostration in which pilgrims bow in respect to their closeness to Allah.

- Mina is a heavenly strip, a profoundly warm embrace where self-sacrifice is experienced together with affection, and the perception of delicacy in obedience to the commands is conducted together with love. Proclaiming, "Learn your rituals from me," our beloved Prophet showed his community how this worship is practiced.

- When Muslims first became an exemplary nation, subject to the guidance of Allah, the leadership of servanthood to Allah was given to the followers of Islam. The change of the *qibla* from Jerusalem to the Ka'ba symbolizes this transfer of leadership. The Messenger of Allah, peace and blessings be upon him, had already sensed this Divine Intention and started to wait in this direction.

- After completing all the rites of hajj in Mecca al-Mukarrama and becoming a *hajji*, a pilgrim normally then goes to Medina al-Munawwara to visit the Masjid an-Nabawi. For the Prophet inspired pilgrims thus: "Whoever visits me after my death, it will be just like he visited me during my life;"[132] "Between my house and my pulpit is a garden from the gardens of Paradise;"[133] and "When a person sends me greeting, Allah returns my soul and I personally receive the greeting of that person and reply to him."[134]

In closing, we plead for all those who will perform the hajj to go and return from the hajj in complete health and safety, and to spend all of their remaining lives in sincere devotion to the pledge they promised to Allah while on this blessed journey. And we beseech them, also, to include us in their prayers while being in those sacred places where all prayers are accepted.

---

[132] Ali al-Kari, Sharh ash-Shifa, 2/149.
[133] Bukhari, Fadail al-Medina, 11; Muslim, Hajj, 502.
[134] Abu Dawud, Manasik, 96.

# Bibliography

Abu Dawud, Sulayman ibn Ash'as ibn Ishaq al-Azdi as-Sijistani, *Sunan*, I–II, Egypt, 1952.

Ajluni, Ismail, ibn Muhammad, *Kashf al-Khafa wa Muzil al-Ilbas, Amma'sh Tahara min al-Ahadith ala as-Sinat an-Nas*, Beirut, third edition, 1988.

Bayhaqi, Abu Bakr Ahmad ibn al-Husayn, *As-Sunan al-Kubra*, I–X, Haydarabad, 1344-1355, ah.

Bilmen, Ömer Nasuhi, *Büyük Islam Ilmihali*, Istanbul: Bilmen Publishing.

Birghiwi, Zaynuddin Muhammad ibn Pir Ali Muhyiddin al-Birghiwi, *At-Tariqat al-Muhammadiyya*, Istanbul, undated.

Bukhari, Abu Abdillah Muhammad ibn Ismail, *Al-Jami as-Sahih*, I–VIII, Istanbul, 1315, ah.

Canan, Ibrahim, *Hadis Ansiklopedisi, Kutub as-Sitta*, I–XVIII, Istanbul: Akçağ Publishing.

Çakan, Ismail Lütfi, *Riyaz as-Salihin*, (*Peygamberimizden Hayat Ölçüleri*, I–VIII), Istanbul: Erkam Publishing.

Darimi, Abu Muhammad Abdullah ibn Abdur Rahman ibn Fadl ibn Bahram, *Sunan ad-Darimi*, I–II, Damascus, 1349 ah.

Davudoğlu, Ahmed, *Sahih-i Müslim Terceme ve Şerhi, I–XI*, Istanbul, undated.

Daylami, Abu Shuja Shirawayh ibn Shardar ibn Shirawayh, *Al-Firdaws bi Ma'thur al-Hitab, I–VI*, Beirut, 1986.

Elmalılı, Muhammed Hamdi Yazır, *Hak Dini Kur'an Dili, I–IX*, Istanbul, undated.

Firuzabadi, Muhammad, ibn Ya'kub, *Al-Qamus al-Muhit*, Beirut, 1987.

Gülen, M. Fethullah, *Asrın Getirdiği Tereddütler, I–IV*, İzmir: Nil Publishing.

———, *Fasıldan Fasıla*, İzmir: Nil Publishing, 1995.

———, *İnancın Gölgesinde*, İzmir: Nil Publishing, 1996.

———, *İnsanlığın İftihar Tablosu, Sonsuz Nur*, İzmir: Nil Publishing, 2000.

———, *Yeşeren Düşünceler*, İzmir: Nil Publishing, 2003.

Hakim, Abu Abdullah Muhammad ibn Abdullah an-Nisaburi, *Al-Mustadrak ala as-Sahihayn, I–IV*, Haydarabad, 1334-1342 ah.

Hamidullah, Muhammad, *Islam Peygamberi*, trns., Istanbul, Irfan Publishing, 1991.

Hatipoğlu, Haydar, *Sünen-i Ibn Mace Terceme ve Şerhi, I–X*, Istanbul, 1982-1983.

Haysami, Nuraddin Ali ibn Abi Bakr, *Majma u'z-Zawaid wa Manba al-Fawaid, I–X*, Cairo, 1352 ah.

Ibn Hajar, Ahmad ibn Ali ibn Hajar al-Askalani, *Hady as-Sari Muqaddima Fath al-Bari*, Beirut, 1993.

Ibn Hanbal, Ahmad, *Musnad, I–IV*, Beirut, undated.

Ibn Hisham, Jamaluddin Abdul Malik, *As-Sirat an-Nabawiyya*, Egypt: Dar al-Ihya at-Turas al-Arabi, undated.

# Bibliography

Ibn Kasir, Abu'l-Fida Ismail ibn al-Hatib Abu Hafs Am ibn Kasir, *Tafsir al-Qur'an al-Azim*, (Edition critique by Muhammad Ibrahim al-Banna, Muhammad Ahmad Ashur, Abdul Aziz Ghunaym, I–VIII), Istanbul, 1984.

\_\_\_\_\_, *Muhtasar at-Tafsir ibn Kasir*, Istanbul: Dar al-Ansar, 1987.

Ibn Maja, Abu Abdillah Muhammad ibn Yazid al-Qazwini, *Sunan*, I–II, Egypt, undated.

Ibn Manzur, Abu Fadl Jamaluddin Muhammad ibn Mukarram ibn Manzur, *Lisan al-Arab*, I–XV, Beirut, undated.

Malik, ibn Anas, Abu Abdillah Malik ibn Anas, *Al-Muwatta*, I–II, Istanbul, 1981.

Mawdudi, Abu al-Ala Mawdudi, *Tafhim al-Qur'an*, trns., Muhammad Han Kayani, I–VII, Istanbul, 1987.

Miras, Kamil, *Tecrid-i Sarih Tercemesi ve Şerhi*, I–XII, Istanbul, 1928-1948.

Muslim, Abu al-Husayn Muslim ibn Hajjaj al-Qushayri an Nisaburi, *Sahih al-Muslim*, I–IV, edition critique by Muhammad Fuad Abdul Baqi, Egypt, 1955.

Naim, Ahmed and Kamil Miras, *Sahih-i Buhari Muhtasarı Tecrid-i Sarih Tercemesi*, I–XII, Ankara, fifth edition, 1979.

Nasai, Abu Abdur Rahman Ahmad ibn Shuayb ibn Ali ibn Bahr ibn Sinan ibn Dinar an-Nasai, *As-Sunan*, I–VIII, Istanbul, 1992.

Nasif, Mansur Ali, *At-Taj al-Jami li al-Usul fi Ahadith ar-Rasul*, I–V, Egypt, 1961.

Necmettin Şahiner, *Son Şahitler*, I–IV, Istanbul: Nesil Publishing.

Nawawi, Abu Zakariyya Yahya ibn Sharaf an-Nawawi, *Al-Minhaj fi Sharh Sahih Muslim Ibn al-Hajjaj*, I–XVIII, second edition, Beirut, 1995.

_____, *Riyaz as-Salihin*, Dar al-Mamun Litturas, 1979.

Nursi, Bediüzzaman Said, *Risale-i Nur Külliyatı ("Risale-i Nur Collection")*, I–II, Istanbul: Nesil Publishing, 1996.

_____, *The Words*, NJ: The Light, 2005.

Öz, Abdullah, *Mekke-Medine Tarihi ve Hac*, Istanbul: Şamil Publishing, 1982.

Qadi 'Iyad ibn Musa al-Yahsubi al-Andulusi, *Ash-Shifa bi Ta'rifi Huquq al-Mustafa*, I–II, Damascus, 1392 ah.

Qurtubi, Abu Abdullah Muhammad ibn Ahmad al-Ansari al-Qurtubi, *Al-Jami li Ahkam al-Qur'an*, I–IX, Cairo, undated.

Shafii, Muhammad ibn Idris ash-Shafii, *Ar-Risala*, Cairo, 1969.

Shatibi, Abu Ishaq Ibrahim ibn Musa ibn Muhammad al-Lahami ash-Shatibi al-Gharniti, *Al-I'tisam*, undated.

_____, *Al-Muwafaqat*, trns. Mehmet Erdoğan, Istanbul, 1990-1993.

Suhayli, Abdur Rahman, *Ar-Rawd al-Unf*, I–VIII, edition critique by Abdur Rahman Wakil, Cairo, 1967.

Suyuti, Jalaluddin Abdur Rahman ibn Abi Bakr as-Suyuti, *Al Jami as-Saghir fi Ahadith al-Bashir wa'n-Nazir*, I–II, Beirut, 1981.

Tirmidhi, Abu Isa Muhammad ibn Isa ibn Sawra at-Tirmidhi, *Al-Jami as-Sahih*, edition critique by Abdul Wahhab Ubayd al-Latif, I–V, Cairo, 1964.

Ünal, Ali, *The Qur'an with Annotated Interpretation in Modern English*, NJ: The Light, 2006.

Zahabi, Abu Abdillah Muhammad ibn Ahmad ibn Uthman ibn Qaymaz, *Siyar A'lam an-Nubala*, I–XXV, edition critique by Şuayb Arnavut, Beirut, 1981-1988.

Zuhayli, Wahba, *At-Tafsir al-Munir*, Beirut: Dar al-Fikr, 1991.

_____, *Islam Fıkhi Ansiklopedisi, ("Encyclopedia of Islamic Jurisprudence")* I–X, Istanbul: Feza Publishing, 1994.